CHINESE
cooking for the Indian kitchen

Nita Mehta
M.Sc. (Food and Nutrition), Gold Medalist

SNAB
Publishers Pvt. Ltd.

Nita Mehta's

CHINESE Cooking For The Indian Kitchen

Second Paperback Edition 2000, 3rd Print 2003

ISBN 81-86004-89-0

Food Styling & Photography: SNAB

Layout and laser typesetting:

N.I.T.A.
☎ 3252948
National Information Technology Academy
3A/3, Asaf Ali Road
New Delhi-110002

Published by:

SNAB
Publishers Pvt Ltd
3A/3 Asaf Ali Road
New Delhi-110002

Editorial and Marketing office:
E-348, Greater Kailash-II, N.Delhi-48
Fax: 91-11-6235218 *Tel:* 91-11-6214011, 6238727
E-Mail: nitamehta@email.com
snab@snabindia.com

The Best of Cookery Books
Website: http://www.nitamehta.com
Website: http://www.snabindia.com

Printed at:
THOMSON PRESS (INDIA) LMITED

Distributed by:
THE VARIETY BOOK DEPOT
A.V.G. Bhavan, M 3 Con Circus
New Delhi - 110 001
Tel: 3327175, 3322567; Fax: 3714335

Price: Rs. 189/-

Contents

Important Tips

- A Chinese dish will have all the vegetables and meat cut in the same shape, e.g. to prepare any dish with noodles, all the vegetables are always cut into thin long strips. For fried rice, everything is diced — cut into small squares.
- Chinese food is crunchy and full of flavour, so never over cook food.
- Always use a big pan or wok to stir-fry. This avoids mashing or breaking the food into bits.
- Use ajinomoto, the Chinese salt, sparingly. Usually just a pinch is enough. When you double the quantity of the dish, do not double the quantity of ajinomoto.
- The amount of soya sauce can be increased or reduced according to the desired colour of the dish. Remember, soya sauce is salty, so keep a check on the salt when you increase the quantity of soya sauce.
- An important tip while preparing chicken soup is that the stock used must always be prepared by boiling chicken with an onion in water.
- Meat used should be of the highest quality.
- Fish used should always be fresh. Ginger and garlic are invariably used in cooking most fish as this helps a great deal in eliminating the so called fishy smell.
- Young birds should be bought when chicken is used, as the cooking time is usually short. Chicken stock is used in almost all the non vegetarian dishes in place of water.
- Rice or noodles form the staple food of the Chinese. Long grained rice is preferred. Always add noodles or rice to boiling water. When rice is cooked, drain the rice and cool before making fried rice. Noodles when cooked should be drained and washed under running tap water. Rub oil over the noodles so that they don't stick to each other.
- Always serve green chillies in vinegar and chilli sauce as accompaniments with the food.

Ingredients used for Chinese Dishes

Bean Sprouts: These are shoots of moong beans or soya beans. The texture is crisp. Bean sprouts are a rich source of vitamins and minerals. To make bean sprouts at home, soak ½ cup of green beans (saboot moong dal) for about 8 hours. Discard water and tie in a muslin cloth. Keep them tied for 2-3 days, remembering to wet the cloth each day. When the shoots are long enough, wash carefully in water. Fresh bean sprouts will keep for several days if refrigerated in a perforated plastic bag.

Chilli Oil: Can be bought ready-made. It can also be made by putting 2 tbsp of chilli powder in a cup and pouring heated oil over it. Use the oil that floats.

Chilli Sauce: This is a hot, spicy and tangy sauce made from chillies and vinegar.

Chinese Wine: There are many kinds of wine made from rice. Chinese wine can be substituted by ordinary dry sherry.

Agar-Agar: This is a dried seaweed. The white fibrous strands require soaking and are used like gelatine. It is used for puddings and as a setting agent.

Cornflour: This is used to thicken sauces. Dissolve some cornflour in little water to make a paste and add it to the boiling liquid. Remember to stir the sauce continuously, when the cornflour paste is being added.

Ajinomoto (Monosodium Glutamate): A white crystalline substance commonly known as MSG. It is used in Chinese cookery for enhancing the flavour of dishes.

Mushrooms: There are many varieties which are used in Chinese cooking. To prepare dried mushrooms for cooking, soak them in hot water for ½ hour to soften.

Bamboo Shoots: Fresh tender shoots of bamboo plant are available rarely, but tinned bamboo shoots are easily available in the big stores.

Bean Curd or Tofu: Bean Curd or Tofu is prepared from soya bean milk and resembles the Indian Paneer in taste and looks. I have thus substituted it with paneer to give you a few exciting delicacies.

Noodles: Dried thin and thick noodles are made with and without eggs. They are usually cooked in boiling water till just done, before frying. Never overcook the noodles. Some varieties of rice noodles are soaked in warm water & then stir fried.

Sesame Oil: An aromatic oil produced from sesame seeds *(til ka tel)*. Adds flavour to dips, sauces, salads and soups.

Soya Sauce: There are two kinds. One is dark and the other is light. Both are used for flavouring soups, stir fried dishes and for seasoning all Chinese foods.

Spring Onions: These are sometimes called scallions or green onions and are used extensively in Chinese cooking. The green part is also used.

Vinegar: Chinese vinegars are made from fermented rice.

Chinese Cooking Methods

PARBOILING:

Parboiling is done when cooking ingredients differ in tenderness and texture. The tougher varieties are added to boiling stock or water for a short time. They are then refreshed in iced water to set color and prevent overcooking. When the parboiled foods are cooked with more tender raw ingredients, the cooking time will then be the same. Whole carrots are peeled, beans are threaded and dropped in boiling water for ½ minute to parboil them. They are then cooled and cut into desired shapes.

STIR-FRYING:

Stir frying food, is to cook food on a high flame for a short period, stirring continuously. Ingredients are added to the wok in order of texture and cooking time. Stir frying of vegetables is done in sequence of their tenderness. E.g. onions are stir fried first, then french beans, then carrots, cabbage and so on. Each vegetable is stir fried for a few seconds, before adding the next vegetable. Ajinomoto is added during stir frying, as it helps to cook the vegetables faster, thus keeping the vegetables crunchy. Stir-frying requires good temperature control and is easily learned through practice. The heat should be progressively raised for the addition of other ingredients. This is used for tender cuts of pork, poultry, seafood and vegetables. The ingredients are sliced, shredded, diced or minced, then stir fried in a wok using a spatula. Before you start stir-frying, remember to —

- Collect all ingredients required for the recipe.
- Slice meat, poultry and seafood. Arrange in order of cooking. Marinate food if required, well in time.
- Measure liquids like oil, sauces and stocks.
- Blend any thickening agent with stock or water and stir before adding to the wok.

DEEP FRYING:

Ingredients are cut into even-sized pieces and dipped into a batter such as flour, beaten egg or bread crumbs. These are immersed in hot oil to cover, until cooked.

- A slice of ginger can be added to indicate the oil's temperature for deep frying. If the ginger turns golden, the oil is right for deep frying.
- Marinated ingredients should be drained before dipping into batter for frying.
- Add small quantities of ingredients to the oil at one time. This maintains the oil's temperature.
- Add some fresh oil to used oil before reusing. This prevents oil from discolouring.

Vegetable fried rice: Recipe on page 117 ➤

Cottage cheese in garlic sauce: Recipe on page 95 ➤

Accompaniments & Sauces

Green Chilli Sauce

Makes 1½ cups

125 gm green chillies
1½ cups white vinegar
1 tsp salt
1 tsp sugar
3-4 cloves *(laung)*

1. Remove stems from whole green chillies.
2. Pressure cook chillies with all the other ingredients to give 3-4 whistles. Cool.
3. Blend in a mixer to a smooth sauce.

Red Chilli Sauce

Makes ¼ cup

4 level tsp red chilli powder
¼ cup vinegar
½ tsp sugar
¼ tsp garam masala
½ tsp salt

1. Mix all ingredients. Cook on medium heat till it reaches the right consistency of a sauce.

Sweet & Sour Sauce

Makes 1½ cups

½ cup tomato ketchup
¼ cup vinegar
2 tbsp sugar
1 cup water
2 tbsp cornflour
½ tsp white pepper
½ tsp salt, or to taste

1. Mix all the ingredients in a pan. Cook, stirring constantly till it boils. Simmer for 2 minutes on low heat. Remove from heat.

Garlic Sauce

Makes 1 cup

15 flakes garlic or 2 tsp garlic paste
1 tbsp oil
2 tbsp tomato ketchup, 1 tsp soya sauce
3/4 cup water
½ tsp white pepper, ½ tsp salt
1 tbsp cornflour mixed with ¼ cup water
a pinch of sugar, ¼ tsp ajinomoto (optional)

1. Peel and grind the garlic to a smooth paste.
2. Heat oil and fry the garlic on low heat till it starts to change it's colour.
3. Add tomato ketchup, pepper, salt and soya sauce. Cook for 1 minute. Add sugar and ajinomoto.
4. Add water. Bring to a boil and simmer for 2 minutes.
5. Add cornflour paste, stirring all the time, until the sauce thickens. Remove from heat.
6. Pour the sauce into a bowl.

Hot Garlic Sauce

Makes 1 cup

20 flakes garlic or 1 tbsp garlic paste
3-4 dry, whole red chillies
2 tbsp oil
2 tbsp tomato ketchup, 1 tsp soya sauce
a pinch of ajinomoto (optional)
½ tsp white pepper, ½ tsp salt, a pinch of sugar
1 tbsp cornflour mixed with 1 cup water

1. Break the red chillies into small pieces.
2. Peel the garlic and grind to a smooth paste along with the red chillies.
3. Heat oil and fry the garlic-chilli paste for 1 minute on low heat.
4. Add tomato ketchup, soya sauce, salt, pepper, ajinomoto and sugar. Cook for ½ minute on low heat.
5. Add cornflour paste, stirring continuously. Boil for 2 minutes till the sauce thickens. Remove the pan from heat and pour the sauce into a bowl.

Ginger Sauce

Makes 1 cup

1 tbsp ginger paste
1 tsp garlic paste - optional
2 tbsp tomato ketchup, 1 tsp soya sauce
1 tbsp oil
1 tbsp cornflour mixed with 1 cup water
½ tsp white pepper, ¼ tsp salt, or to taste
½ tsp sugar

1. Heat oil and fry the ginger and garlic paste for 2 minutes over a low flame.
2. Add tomato ketchup, soya sauce, salt, pepper and sugar. Cook for 1 minute.
3. Reduce flame and add cornflour paste, stirring continuously. Simmer for 2 minutes on low heat till thick.
4. Remove pan from fire and pour the sauce into a bowl.

Hot & Sour Sauce

Makes 3/4 cup

3/4 cup water, 2 tbsp vinegar
1 tsp black pepper powder, salt to taste
1 tbsp cornflour, ½ tsp sugar

1. Mix all the ingredients in a pan. Cook, stirring constantly till it boils. Simmer for 2 minutes on low heat. Remove from fire.

Green Chillies in Vinegar

Makes ¼ cup

¼ cup white vinegar
½ tsp salt, ½ tsp sugar
2-3 drops soya sauce, 2-3 green chillies

1. Chop green chillies finely.
2. Mix all the other ingredients. Add green chillies.
3. Heat on fire till it is just about to boil.
4. Remove from fire. Serve in a small bowl.

Starters

Vegetable Gold Coin

Serves 12 *Picture on back cover*

6 bread slices
2 small potatoes - boiled
1 spring onion - chopped finely upto the greens (keep greens separate)
1 carrot - chopped finely
1 capsicum - chopped finely
2 tsp soya sauce
½ tsp pepper
¼ tsp chilli powder
¼ tsp ajinomoto (optional)
salt to taste
¼ cup plain flour *(maida)* dissolved in ¼ cup water
1 tbsp white sesame seeds (*til*)
oil for frying

1. Grate boiled potatoes.
2. Heat 1½ tbsp oil. Add only the white part of spring onions. Cook for a minute, till transparent.
3. Add vegetables and the green onions. Cook for 3-4 minutes on low flame.
4. Add potatoes, soya sauce, salt, pepper & chilli powder. Cook for 2-3 minutes. Keep aside.
5. With a cutter or a sharp lid of a bottle, cut out small rounds (about 1½" diameter) of the bread.
6. Spread some potato mixture in a heap on the round piece of bread in the centre leaving ¼" edges of the bread. Press.
7. Spread plain flour paste over the potato mixture taking care to apply the paste nicely on the edges of the potato dome, so as to join the potatoes with the bread.
8. Sprinkle sesame seeds. Press gently.
9. Deep fry in hot oil. Turn sides quickly as the bread turns brown very fast. Serve hot, dotted with chilli-garlic sauce.

Fried Vegetable Wontons

Serves 6

WONTONS WRAPPERS
2 cups plain flour *(maida)*
½ tsp salt
oil for deep frying

WONTON STUFFING
3/4 cup boiled noodles
2 cups cabbage - finely chopped
2 onions - finely chopped
1 carrot - grated
3/4 cup bean sprouts
½ tsp ajinomoto powder (optional)
2 tsp soya sauce
salt and black pepper to taste
2 tbsp oil

1. To prepare the wonton wrappers, sieve the plain flour and salt together.
2. Add hot water gradually and make a soft dough. Knead well till smooth and keep aside for 30 minutes.
3. Knead the dough with oiled hands until it becomes smooth and elastic.
4. To prepare the stuffing, heat oil in a wok or a frying pan on a high flame. Add the cabbage, onions, carrot, bean sprouts and ajinomoto and stir fry over a high flame for 3 minutes.
5. Add the noodles, soya sauce and salt. Keep stuffing aside.
6. Roll out the wrapper dough into thin circles of about 2½" diameter.
7. Put a little stuffing in the centre of each dough circle and fold over to make a semicircle. Bring the ends together and press.
8. Repeat with the remaining dough and stuffing.
9. Deep fry the wontons in oil to a golden brown. Serve with green chilli and garlic sauce.

Golden Fried Prawns

Serves 4

(250 gms) 12 large prawns - cleaned & deveined
1 tbsp sesame seeds *(til)*

MARINADE
1 tbsp soya sauce
1 tbsp wine or sherry
¼ tsp ajinomoto (optional)
½ tsp salt
¼ tsp black pepper

BATTER
1 egg
3 tbsp plain flour *(maida)*
3 tbsp cornflour
3/4 tsp baking powder
1 tbsp oil
¼ tsp white pepper
¼ tsp salt
¼ tsp ajinomoto (optional)

1. In a bowl mix soya sauce, sherry, ajinomoto, salt & black pepper. Marinate the prawns in it for 15-30 minutes.
2. Make a smooth paste by adding plain flour, cornflour, baking powder, oil, salt, white pepper & ajinomoto to the egg. Add just enough water to get a very thick batter such that it is of a coating consistency.
3. Dip the prawns into the batter.
4. Sprinkle sesame seeds on the prawns and deep fry one to two pieces at a time, till golden brown.
5. Serve hot with chilli sauce.

Note : *If desired you can let the tail remain and then marinate the prawns.*

Chicken Spring Rolls

Picture on facing page **Serves 4-6**

WRAPPINGS
1 egg
4 tbsp plain flour *(maida)*
4 tbsp cornflour
½ cup water, approx.
¼ tsp salt

FILLING
1 tbsp chopped ginger
250 gms chicken boneless - boiled and shredded
1 cup shredded cabbage
½ cup shredded carrots
½ cup shredded onions
½ cup shredded capsicum
½ cup bean sprouts
1 tsp salt
a pinch of ajinomoto (optional)
1 tbsp soya sauce

1. To prepare the filling, heat 1 tbsp oil in a pan.
2. Add chopped ginger. Saute till it starts changing colour.
3. Add the chicken and the remaining vegetables. Stir fry for 2 minutes.
4. Add salt, ajinomoto and soya sauce.
5. Remove from heat and put in a strainer so that excess water flows out. Allow the filling to cool.
6. To prepare the wrappings, sift together plain flour and cornflour. Add salt, egg and mix well. Add enough water gradually to get a thin pouring consistency.
7. Pour 2 tbsp batter on a moderately hot nonstick tawa, spread the batter by tilting the pan and make pancakes. Do not cook on the other side. Make all pancakes in this way and pile on a plate. Cover with a damp cloth.
8. Put 2 tbsp of filling on the cooked side of a pancake.
9. Moisten the edges with flour paste. Fold ½ " from the other two sides to seal the filling and roll up.
10. Arrange rolls in a tray and cover with cling film. If you chill for ½ hour, it will keep a better shape.
11. Deep fry over a medium heat until golden brown and crisp. Drain on absorbent paper. Cut into 3 or 4 pieces. Serve hot with chilli sauce.

Corn Rolls

Makes 20 rolls

10 fresh bread slices - sides removed
2 tbsp plain flour *(maida)* dissolved in 2 tbsp water to make a paste
oil for deep frying

FILLING

1 cup canned sweet corn - cream style
1 spring onion - chopped upto the greens
1 green chilli - finely chopped
1½ tsp soya sauce
¼ tsp ajinomoto (optional)
2 tbsp oil
salt and pepper to taste
chilli sauce to serve

1. Heat the oil and stir fry the spring onion and green chilli for ½ minute.
2. Add the sweet corn, soya sauce, ajinomoto, salt and pepper. Mix well and cook till the mixture becomes dry. Cool.
3. Microwave the bread for a few seconds and roll out with a rolling pin so that it becomes thinner. If the bread is not fresh, rolling might be a problem.
4. Spread a little filling and roll into a cylinder shape tightly.
5. Seal the end of the roll with a little plain flour paste.
6. Deep fry in oil until golden brown.
7. Cut each roll into two vertically. Serve with chilli sauce.

Fried Chicken Wontons

Serves 4

STUFFING
100 gms cooked chicken mince
1 tbsp chopped spring onions
salt to taste
½ tsp ajinomoto (optional)
2 egg whites - beaten

DOUGH
1 cup plain flour *(maida)*
2 tbsp cornflour
2 eggs
water - for kneading the dough
oil for frying

1. Make a tight dough using plain flour, cornflour, eggs and water. Keep in a cool place covered with a damp cloth for 30 minutes.
2. Mix all the ingredients of the stuffing together.
3. Take out the dough and roll out flat, as thin as possible. Cut square sheets — 2½" x 2½".
4. Put a little stuffing in the centre and seal the sides using egg. Give it a boat shape or a bag shape with the stuffing in the centre.
5. Deep fry in hot oil till golden brown. Drain.
6. Serve hot with tomato ketchup or chilli sauce.

Vegetable Spring Rolls

Serves 4

PANCAKES
½ cup plain flour *(maida)*, 1 cup milk
a pinch of soda-bicarb, ¼ tsp salt
oil for shallow frying

FILLING
1 onion - chopped finely
8 french beans - parboiled
½ carrot - shredded
½ cup shredded cabbage, ½ cup shredded capsicum
½ cup bean sprouts
a pinch of ajinomoto (optional)
½ tsp white pepper, ½ tsp sugar, salt to taste
1 tsp soya sauce
2 tbsp oil

1. To prepare the pancakes, sift plain flour and salt. Add milk gradually, beating well to make a smooth thin batter. Add soda-bicarb. Mix well.
2. Heat a nonstick pan, taking care not to heat it too much. Smear 1 tsp oil on it.
3. Remove the pan from fire and pour half the batter on it. Tilt the pan to spread the batter evenly. Return to heat.
4. Remove the pancake from the pan when the underside is cooked. Do not cook the other side.
5. Make the other pancake also in the same way.
6. Cool the two pancakes on a dry cloth, keeping the cooked side on top.
7. To prepare the filling, parboil beans. String french beans and drop whole into boiling water with ½ tsp salt for ½ minute. Strain. Then shred diagonally.
8. Heat oil. Add onions and sprouts & stir fry for 1 minute. Add ajinomoto, salt, pepper & sugar.
9. Add all other vegetables. Stir fry for 1 minute. Add soya sauce and mix well.
10. Place half of the filling on the cooked side of the pancake, at one end which is nearest to you.
11. Fold ½" from the left side and then the right side. Roll upwards.
12. Seal the edges with cornflour paste, made by dissolving 1 tsp of cornflour in 1 tsp of water. If you chill for ½ hour, it keeps better shape.
13. Heat some oil in a pan. Shallow fry both sides of the roll till golden brown. Drain on absorbent paper. Cut diagonally into 1" pieces. Serve hot.

Paper Fried Chicken

Serves 4-6

butter paper - cut into 6" x 6" squares

FILLING
200 gms shredded raw chicken (boneless)
2-3 flakes of garlic - crushed, ¼ tsp crushed ginger
¼ tsp each of salt, pepper, sugar, ajinomoto (optional)
1 tbsp soy sauce, 1 tbsp sherry or gin
1 tbsp cornflour
1 egg

1. Mix all the above ingredients of the filling together.
2. Divide the filling into 6 portions. Place one portion of the filling on one side of the square piece of butter paper. Roll upwards to get a long roll. Push the sides of the paper to seal the filling.
3. Deep fry with the paper to brown before serving. Arrange in a flat serving dish along with the paper and garnish with shredded lettuce leaves.

Marbled Eggs

Serves 6-8

6-8 eggs
3 tbsp tea leaves
1" cinnamon stick *(dalchini)*
3 star anise
3 tbsp soya sauce

1. Boil eggs for 10 minutes until hard boiled.
2. Drain and cool at once by placing in iced water.
3. Tap each egg with the back of a spoon until cracks appear all over.
4. Take enough water in a pan and put the eggs in it, such that the eggs are covered with water.
5. Keep the pan on fire and add tea leaves, cinnamon stick, stir anise and soya sauce.
6. Simmer gently on low flame for at least ½ hour. Allow to cool and shell before serving. Serve along with chilli sauce.

Stuffed Egg Fuyong

Serves 6

6 eggs
salt and black pepper powder - to taste
oil to fry

FILLING
100 gms finely chopped chicken pieces
50 gms button mushrooms - chopped
50 gms prawns - cleaned, deveined & chopped
1 tsp rice wine or sherry
1 tsp soya sauce
½ tsp sugar
½ tsp chopped ginger
2 spring onions - chopped finely (diced)

1. Beat eggs and season with salt and pepper. Keep aside.
2. Mix chicken, prawns and mushrooms together in a bowl.
3. Add wine, soya sauce, sugar and ginger. Add salt and pepper to taste. Mix in spring onions. Keep filling aside.
4. Heat wok and add 1 tsp oil.
5. Spoon 3 tbsp of the beaten egg and spread in a circle of 3-4" diameter.
6. Spoon 2 tsp filling in the centre of the egg.
7. When underside of the egg sets, fold the egg circle over to make a crescent (half moon) shape. Press gently.
8. Cook for 2-3 minutes on low heat to cook the filling.
9. Make the remaining pancakes in the same way. Serve with chilli sauce.

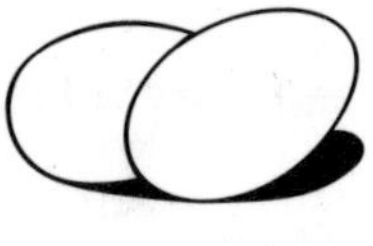

Chinese Potato Rolls

Serves 8

ROLLS

4 medium potatoes - boiled & mashed well
3 tbsp cornflour
1 green chilli - deseeded & chopped
2 tbsp coriander - chopped
3/4 tsp salt
½ tsp pepper

SAUCE

1 tbsp oil
6-8 flakes garlic - crushed
1 green chilli - deseeded and chopped
2 tbsp tomato ketchup
1½ tbsp soya sauce
1 tsp red chilli sauce
¼ tsp pepper
¼ tsp salt
2 tbsp coriander - chopped
1 tsp cornflour dissolved in 1/3 cup water

1. Mash and mix potatoes with all the ingredients of the rolls.
2. With wet hands, shape into small rolls, of about 1" size. Make the sides flat.
3. Deep fry in medium hot oil to golden brown. Keep aside.
4. For the sauce, heat 1 tbsp oil in a pan. Reduce flame. Add garlic and green chillies.
5. When garlic changes colour, remove from fire.
6. Add tomato ketchup, chilli sauce and soya sauce. Return to fire and add salt, pepper. Cook the sauces for ½ minute.
7. Add cornflour dissolved in water. Add chopped coriander.
8. Simmer for a minute till thick.
9. Add the fried rolls and stir till the sauce coats the rolls, for about 1 minute. Serve hot.

Note : *Advance work can be done upto step 7, but thicken the sauce and add the rolls to the sauce at the time of serving. If the rolls are in the sauce for too long, they turn limp.*

Chilli Paneer with Green Peppers

Picture on page 2

Serves 4

1½ tbsp cornflour
1½ tbsp plain flour *(maida)*
½ tsp salt
150 gms paneer
1 yellow and 1 green pepper *(capsicum)* or
2 green peppers - cut into 3/4" pieces
2 tsp soya sauce
1½ tbsp tomato ketchup
½ tbsp vinegar
4-5 green chillies - slit lengthwise
4-5 flakes crushed garlic - optional
1 tbsp coriander - chopped
¼ tsp each of ajinomoto (optional)
¼ tsp each of salt, pepper, sugar
a few tooth picks

1. Mix plain flour, cornflour and salt. Add enough water, about 3 tbsp, to make a batter of a thick pouring consistency, such that it coats the paneer.
2. Cut paneer into 3/4" cubes.
3. Dip each piece in the batter and deep fry to a golden brown colour. Keep aside.
4. Heat 2 tbsp oi in a panl. Fry the green chillies and garlic. Reduce heat. Add salt, pepper, sugar and ajinomoto.
5. Add soya sauce, chilli sauce, tomato ketchup and vinegar. Stir.
6. Add green peppers. Stir fry for a few seconds.
7. Add the fried paneer and coriander. Mix well. Remove from heat.
8. To serve, on a tooth pick, thread a piece of capsicum, then a paneer and again a piece of capsicum.

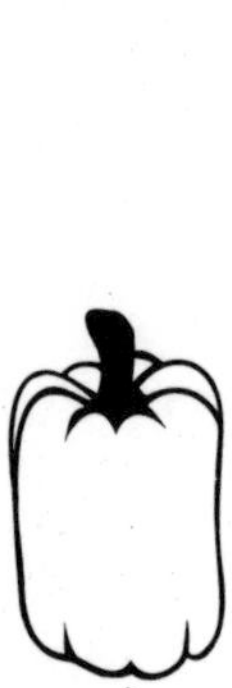

Sesame Fingers

Serves 10-12

6 bread slices
¼ cup plain flour *(maida)* dissolved in ¼ cup water to make a paste
2 tbsp sesame seeds *(til)*

TOPPING
2 boiled potatoes - grated
1 onion - chopped finely
2 carrots - chopped finely
¼ of a small cabbage or 1 large capsicum - chopped finely
1 small bunch coriander - chopped finely (½ cup)
½ tsp pepper
½ tsp chilli powder
2 tsp soya sauce
salt to taste
2 tbsp oil

1. Heat oil. Add onions. Cook till transparent.
2. Add carrots & cabbage, cook for 2-3 minutes.
3. Add boiled potatoes.
4. Add salt, pepper to taste and soya sauce. Cook for 2-3 minutes. Add coriander. Mix. Remove from fire.
5. Put some vegetable mixture on a bread slice.
6. Press well. Apply plain flour paste on the vegetables.
7. Sprinkle sesame seeds generously. Press a little.
8. Fry in hot oil till bread is golden brown.
9. Cut bread slices into four thin fingers. Serve hot.

Soups

Chicken Stock for Soups

Makes 10 cups

½ kg chicken - cleaned (keep whole or cut into 8 big pieces)
1 onion - grated or sliced
1 tsp crushed garlic, 1 tsp crushed ginger
1 tsp salt
12 cups of water

1. Put all the ingredients in a cooker. Pressure cook for 15 minutes.
2. Cool and remove the meat from the bones. (This meat can be used in soups, fried rice, noodles).
3. Add the bones to the liquid in the cooker along with 1 cup of water and cook for another 10 minutes.
4. Strain and use the stock for soups and sauces.

Note : *Stock can be made in advance and frozen in the freezer compartment and used when required.*

Vegetable Stock for Soups

Makes 6 cups

1 onion - chopped
1 carrot - chopped, 1 potato - chopped
4-5 french beans - chopped
or
½ cup chopped cabbage
½ tsp crushed garlic - optional
1 tsp crushed ginger, ½ tsp salt
7 cups water

1. Mix all ingredients and pressure cook for 10-15 minutes.
2. Do not mash the vegetables if a clear soup is to be prepared. Strain and use as required.

Note : *Soup cubes or seasoning cubes may be boiled with water and used instead of the stock, if you are short of time.*

Hot & Sour Chicken Soup

Serves 4

1 breast of chicken - shredded
1 tbsp oil
2 tbsp shredded mushrooms
2 tbsp shredded bamboo shoots (optional)
4 tbsp shredded cabbage
3 tbsp carrot - shredded
leaves of 1 spring onion - finely cut
5 cups chicken stock (page 31)
2 tbsp soya sauce
3 tbsp lime juice or vinegar
1 tsp black pepper
½ tbsp salt
½ tbsp sugar
½ tsp ajinomoto (optional)
4 tbsp cornflour
1 egg - lightly beaten
1 tsp sesame oil or sunflower oil
1 tsp chilli powder

1. Heat 1 tbsp oil in a pan.
2. Add the vegetables (except leaves of spring onions) and saute for a minute.
3. Add the stock and give it 2-3 boils.
4. Reduce heat and add soya sauce, vinegar/lime juice, salt, sugar, ajinomoto & pepper.
5. Add spring onion leaves.
6. Mix cornflour with ½ cup water. Add to the soup, stirring constantly.
7. Bring to a boil. Gradually pour in lightly beaten egg, stirring the soup continuously with a fork to get shreds of egg. Remove from fire.
8. In a spoon heat sesame or sunflower oil. Remove from fire. Add chilli powder. Add the chilli oil to the soup.
9. Cover soup immediately for a few minutes. Serve hot.

Sizzling Vegetable Soup

Serves 4

5 cups vegetable stock - (page 31)
10 spinach leaves - torn into two pieces
1 carrot - sliced diagonally
a few mushrooms - whole
100 gms tofu or paneer - cut into 1" cubes
100 gms puffed rice *(chirwa)* - fried to a golden colour
1 tsp salt
½ tsp ajinomoto (optional)
¼ tsp pepper
1 tsp sherry - optional
1 tbsp soya sauce

1. Prepare vegetable stock as given on page 31. Bring stock to a boil.
2. Add spinach, carrots and mushrooms to the boiling stock. Cook for 5-7 minutes.
3. Add tofu or paneer.
4. Mix in salt, pepper and ajinomoto.
5. Add soya sauce and keep aside.
6. At the time of serving, mix in the puffed rice lightly.
7. Serve with chilli sauce.

Hot & Sour Vegetable Soup

Picture on facing page ***Serves 6***

TOMATO STOCK
6 cups water
2 big tomatoes

OTHER INGREDIENTS
2 tbsp oil
1 tomato - chopped very fine
½ cup chopped cabbage
½ cup grated carrot
1 tbsp finely cut french beans
1-2 tbsp dried mushrooms - soaked for ½ hour (optional)
½ tsp ajinomoto (optional)
½ tsp sugar
1 level tsp black pepper powder
1½ tsp chilli sauce
1 tsp soya sauce
1½ tbsp vinegar
4 tbsp cornflour mixed with ½ cup water
50 gms tofu or paneer - diced (cut into tiny cubes), optional

1. Pressure cook water and tomatoes together to give 2-3 whistles. Strain. Keep the tomato stock aside.
2. If dried mushrooms are available, soak them in water for ½ hour to soften.
3. Heat oil. Add chopped tomato. Mash while cooking it. Cook for 1 minute.
4. Add cabbage, carrot, soaked mushrooms and beans. Stir fry for 1 minute.
5. Add the prepared tomato stock.
6. Add all the other ingredients except cornflour paste. Boil for 2 minutes.
7. Add cornflour paste, stirring continuously. Cook for 2-3 minutes till the soup turns thick.
8. Add diced tofu or paneer. Serve hot, accompanied with green chillies in vinegar.

Vegetable Sweet Corn Soup
(with Fresh Corn)

Picture on back cover ***Serves 6***

4 big whole corns-on-the cob
½ tsp ajinomoto (optional)
4 level tbsp cornflour dissolved in 1 cup water
2-3 tbsp sugar
salt to taste
½ tsp white pepper
1-2 tbsp white vinegar
½ cup cabbage - shredded
½ cup carrots - very finely chopped

1. Take out a few whole corn kernels and grate the rest of the corn on the grater.
2. Pressure cook corn with 6 cups of water and 2 tsp salt.
3. After the first whistle, keep on low heat for 15 minutes. Remove from heat.
4. After the pressure drops, mix cornflour in water and add to cooked corn.
5. Add sugar, ajinomoto, vinegar and pepper.
6. Give it one boil. Keep it boiling for 8-10 minutes. More cornflour, dissolved in a little water may be added if the soup appears thin.
7. Add the vegetables — cabbage and carrot.
8. After adding the vegetables, boil the soup for 2-3 minutes only. Do not overcook the vegetables, leave them crunchy and crisp.
9. Serve hot with green chillies in vinegar.

Vegetable Sweet Corn Soup
(with Tinned Corn)

Serves 6-8 *Picture on back cover*

1 tin (450 gm) sweet corn - cream style
1½ tbsp vinegar
½ tsp ajinomoto (optional)
2½ tsp salt, or to taste
½ tsp white pepper
5 cups water
4 level tbsp cornflour dissolved in 1 cup of water
½ tsp sugar (optional)

1. Open the corn tin. Churn the corn just for a second in a grinder, so that most of the corn kernels are roughly crushed, and a few corns are left whole too.
2. Mix corn and water in a pan. Boil for 3-4 minutes.
3. Add vinegar, ajinomoto, sugar, salt and pepper.
4. Mix cornflour in water and add to the soup, stirring continuously.
5. Cook for 8-10 minutes, stirring occasionally.
6. More cornflour may be dissolved in a little water and added to the boiling soup, if the soup appears thin. Boil for 3-4 minutes after adding the cornflour paste.
7. Serve hot with green chillies in vinegar.

Tomato Egg Drop Coriander Soup

Serves 4

3 cups chicken stock (page 31)
4 tomatoes - deseeded and cut into slices
1 tbsp tomato ketchup
2 tsp soya sauce
salt to taste
½ tsp ajinomoto (optional)
2-3 tbsp chopped and washed coriander
1 egg - beaten

1. In a wok, bring stock to boil.
2. Add all the ingredients except egg and chopped coriander.
3. Boil together for 1-2 minutes. Reduce heat.
4. Now add the beaten egg and stir immediately with a fork to form threads.
5. Finish with chopped coriander. Serve hot.

Peking Hot & Sour Soup

Serves 4-6

4 dried, Chinese mushrooms - soaked in warm water for 20 minutes
4 cups chicken stock (page 31)
100 gms lean pork - shredded
¼ cup canned bamboo shoots - shredded (optional)
100 gm tofu or paneer - cut into ½" squares
3 tbsp white vinegar, 1 tbsp soya sauce
1½ tbsp cornflour mixed with 1/3 cup water
1 egg - beaten, ½ tsp sesame oil
3 green onions - chopped

1. Squeeze mushrooms dry and remove stems. Cut mushroom caps into thin strips.
2. Bring stock to a boil and add pork and mushrooms. Bring to a boil again, reduce heat and simmer for 8-10 minutes. Add bamboo shoots and tofu or paneer and simmer for another 4-5 minutes.
3. Mix vinegar and soya sauce and stir into the soup. Stir in blended cornflour and water and simmer, stirring constantly, until thickened.
4. Remove from heat. Add the beaten egg and stir immediately with a fork to form threads. Add sesame oil and green onions and serve hot.

Sizzling Chicken Soup

Serves 4

5 cups chicken stock (page 31)
1 breast of chicken (raw) - cut into 1" squares
2 pieces bamboo shoots - (optional)
1 carrot - sliced
5-6 mushrooms - sliced
10 spinach leaves - cut into halves
1 tsp salt
¼ tsp pepper
½ tsp ajinomoto (optional)
100 gm puffed rice *(chirwa)*
1 tsp sherry
1 tbsp soya sauce
oil for frying puffed rice

1. Slice the carrot, bamboo shoots and mushrooms.
2. Cut the spinach leaves into half. Blanch in hot water for a minute. Remove and put into ice cold water to refresh.
3. Remove the meat from the bones. Cut into 1" square pieces.
4. Heat 1 tbsp oil in a wok. Fry the chicken pieces for 1-2 minutes.
5. Add chicken stock and bring to a boil. Cook for 3-4 minutes.
6. Add vegetables and the blanched spinach. Further cook for 2-3 minutes.
7. Add salt, ajinomoto and soya sauce. Remove from heat. Keep aside.
8. Deep fry puffed rice to a golden brown colour.
9. Serve hot soup, sprinkled with deep fried puffed rice.

Chicken Noodle Soup

Serves 4

½ cup noodles - boiled
5 cups chicken stock (page 31)
1 cooked chicken breast - shredded
1/3 cup cooked ham - shredded
¼ cup fresh mushrooms - cut into paper thin slices
1 carrot - shredded
1 tsp salt
¼ tsp pepper
½ tsp ajinomoto (optional)
spring onions or leeks - for garnishing

1. Boil chicken stock. Add chicken meat, ham, mushrooms and carrots. Boil for 1 minute.
2. Add boiled noodles.
3. Add salt, pepper and ajinomoto.
4. Serve hot garnished with diagonally cut leaves of leeks or spring onions.
5. Serve along with soya sauce, green chillies in vinegar and chilli sauce.

Wonton Vegetable Soup

Serves 6

WONTON WRAPPERS WITHOUT EGGS
1 cup plain flour *(maida)*
½ tsp salt
1 tbsp oil
a little water (chilled)

WONTON FILLING
½ carrot - parboiled and chopped very finely
8 french beans - parboiled and chopped very finely
½ cup cabbage - finely chopped
¼ cup onion - finely chopped
a pinch of ajinomoto (optional)
½ tsp sugar
½ tsp white pepper
1 tsp soya sauce
salt to taste
1 tbsp oil

WONTON SOUP
6 cups vegetable stock - recipe on page 31
2 spring onions - chopped
½ cucumber - thinly sliced
1 tbsp soya sauce
1 tsp white pepper
1 tsp sugar
¼ tsp ajinomoto (optional)

1. To prepare the wonton wrappers, sift plain flour and salt.
2. Rub in oil till the flour resembles bread crumbs.
3. Add chilled water gradually and make a stiff dough.
4. Knead the dough well for about 5 minutes till smooth.
5. Cover the dough with a damp cloth and keep aside for ½ hour.
6. To prepare the filling, heat oil. Stir fry onions, for a few seconds.
2. Add all other vegetables. Stir fry for ½ minute.
3. Add salt, pepper, sugar, soya sauce & ajinomoto. Mix and remove from fire.
4. Cool the filling.
6. Divide the dough into 4 balls. Roll out each ball into thin chappatis.
7. Cut into 2" square pieces. Place a little filling in the centre.

contd ...

8. Lift one corner of a 2" piece and join to the opposite corner to make a triangle. Press the sides to seal the filling.
9. Keeping the pointed end of the triangle down, hold the other two corners.
10. Gently bring them down and join the two corners. Seal with water or cornflour paste.
11. Press the joint nicely to get the wonton shape. The wontons may be folded into different shapes like money bags, nurses caps or envelopes. Keep wontons aside.
12. To prepare the soup, boil vegetable stock.
13. Add the prepared wontons. Cover and cook for 12-15 minutes on low flame till they float on the top.
14. Add all the other ingredients. Simmer for 1-2 minutes. Serve hot.

Lung Fung Soup

Serves 4

3 tbsp oil
¼ cup bean sprouts
¼ cup minced (cut into very tiny pieces) mushrooms (optional)
¼ cup minced bamboo shoots (optional)
½ cup minced carrots
½ cup minced french beans
¼ cup minced capsicum
½ cup chopped coriander leaves
¼ cup tiny florets of cauliflower
½ tsp ajinomoto (optional)
1 tsp white pepper
salt to taste
5 cups water
1 tsp sugar
1 tbsp soya sauce
5 tbsp cornflour mixed with 1 cup water
2 tbsp vinegar

1. Heat oil and stir fry the bean sprouts, mushrooms and bamboo shoots over a high flame for 2 minutes.
2. Add the remaining vegetables, ajinomoto, pepper and salt.
3. Stir fry over a high flame for 2 minutes.
4. Add water, sugar, soya sauce, vinegar and salt.
5. Bring to a boil and simmer uncovered, for 1 minute.
6. Add cornflour mixed with 1 cup water.
7. Bring to a boil, stirring continuously, and simmer uncovered, for 1 minute.

Fish Meat Ball Soup

Serves 4

BALLS
½ kg fish
250 gms minced mutton
¼ tsp ajinomoto (optional)
½ tsp pepper
½ tsp sugar
salt to taste
1½ tsp soya sauce
2 tbsp cornflour
1-2 eggs

SOUP
6 cups water
fish and mutton bones
¼ tsp salt
¼ tsp ajinomoto (optional)
¼ tsp sugar

GARNISHING
1-2 spring onions along with the greens - chopped

1. Clean the fish. Remove the flesh and bones. Mash the flesh.
2. Take minced meat and fish flesh and mix well adding salt, pepper, sugar, ajinomoto, eggs, soya sauce and cornflour.
3. Make small balls of the mixture. Take cold water in a pan and put all the balls in it. Put the pan on fire. When cooked remove and keep aside.
4. Put the fish and meat bones in 6 cups water with salt and cook for 15 minutes. Strain well and remove bones.
5. Add ajinomoto and sugar. Put the balls and cook soup for 2-3 minutes.
6. Check seasonings and sprinkle some spring onions over it and serve hot.

Sweet Corn Chicken Soup

Serves 8

10 cups chicken stock (page 31)
1 tin sweet corn (cream style)
1 cup cooked chicken - shredded
3 tbsp cornflour
2 eggs - beaten lightly
salt and pepper to taste
1 tsp sugar
½ tsp ajinomoto (optional)

1. Pour stock into a pan. Mix in the sweet corn and allow to cook on high heat for 5-7 minutes.
2. Add sugar, ajinomoto, salt and pepper.
3. Mix cornflour in ½ cup water, add to the soup stirring all the time until the soup gets thick.
4. Add the beaten eggs and stir with a fork so that threads are formed.
5. Add the shredded and cooked chicken pieces, keeping a little aside to sprinkle on top of the soup when poured into the bowls.
6. Serve hot along with soya sauce, green chillies in vinegar and chilli sauce.

Mushroom & Bean Sprout Soup

Serves 6

1 cup sliced fresh mushrooms
1 cup bean sprouts
6 cups vegetable stock (page 31) or water with a seasoning cube
1 tbsp soya sauce
1 tbsp vinegar
1 tsp sugar
1 tsp white pepper
salt to taste
¼ tsp ajinomoto (optional)
2 tbsp cornflour dissolved in ¼ cup water
1 tbsp crushed ginger
2 tbsp oil

1. Prepare vegetable stock as given on page 31.
2. Heat oil. Stir fry bean sprouts and mushrooms for 2 minutes.
3. Add crushed ginger. Stir fry for ½ minute.
4. Add vegetable stock or a seasoning cube dissolved in 6 cups of water.
5. Add all the other ingredients except cornflour paste.
6. Boil. Add cornflour paste. Cook for 1 minute till the soup turns thick.
7. Serve hot.

Wonton Chicken Soup

Serves 4

WONTON WRAPPERS
3/4 cup plain flour *(maida)*
1 egg
¼ tsp salt

FILLING
6 tbsp finely chopped cooked chicken/pork
3-4 mushrooms - finely chopped
salt & pepper to taste
¼ tsp ajinomoto (optional)

SOUP
6 cups chicken stock (page 31)
2-3 pieces of bamboo shoots - cut into slices (optional)
1 carrot - cut into slices
2-3 spinach leaves - torn into halves
50 gms cabbage - sliced
1 tsp salt
¼ tsp ajinomoto (optional)

1. Mix all the ingredients of the filling and keep aside.
2. To prepare the wontons, mix all the ingredients of the wontons and knead it into a smooth dough using little water if necessary.
3. Wrap in a polythene and keep in the fridge for ½ hour.
4. Roll out the dough as thin as possible.
5. Cut about 3 inch square pieces.
6. Spread a little egg on the corners of each piece.
7. Put a tsp of filling in the centre. Bring opposite ends together and bind the two ends with egg. Keep wontons aside.
8. Slice the vegetables.
9. In a wok, bring chicken stock to a boil, drop in the wontons. Cover and cook over low heat for 8-10 minutes, till they float on top.
10. Then add the vegetables. Cook for 5-7 minutes. Lastly add ajinomoto and salt.
11. Serve hot with chilli sauce and green chillies in vinegar.

Green Peas Soup

Serves 6

8 cups clear vegetable stock (page 31) or water
1½ cups shelled tender green peas
½ cup finely chopped cabbage
½ cup finely grated carrot
2 pinches of ajinomoto (optional)
2 pinches sugar
¼ tsp black pepper
1 tsp soya sauce
5 level tbsp cornflour dissolved in ½ cup water
2 tbsp oil
salt to taste

1. Prepare stock as given on page 31, if time permits. Boil stock or water. Add peas. Cook till tender. Keep aside.
2. Heat oil. Add cabbage, carrot and ajinomoto. Stir fry over a high flame for ½ minute.
3. Add the stock with peas. Add sugar, pepper powder and salt. Add soya sauce.
4. Mix the cornflour in ½ cup of water and add this paste to the soup.
5. Cook for about 3 minutes while stirring continuously.
6. Serve hot with chillies in vinegar, soya sauce and chilli sauce.

Talomein Soup

4 cups vegetable stock - recipe on page 31
½ carrot - parboiled and cut into leaves or diagonally cut slices
3-4 cabbage leaves - roughly torn
1 cup boiled noodles
2 tbsp cornflour dissolved in ½ cup water
1 tsp soya sauce
1 tsp salt, or to taste
½ tsp each of sugar, black pepper
a pinch ajinomoto (optional)

1. Mix stock, salt, pepper, sugar, soya sauce and ajinomoto. Boil.
2. Add cornflour paste, stirring continuously.
3. Add vegetables.
4. Boil for 2-3 minutes.
5. Add boiled noodles, remove from fire. Serve.

Chicken Talomein Soup

4 cups chicken stock - recipe on page 31
½ cup cooked shredded chicken
½ carrot - parboiled and cut into leaves or diagonally cut slices
1-2 cabbage leaves - roughly torn
½ cup boiled noodles
2 tbsp cornflour dissolved in ½ cup water
1½ tsp soya sauce
salt to taste
½ tsp each of sugar, black pepper
a pinch ajinomoto (optional)

1. Mix stock, salt, pepper, sugar, soya sauce and ajinomoto. Boil.
2. Add cornflour paste, stirring continuously.
3. Add vegetables and shredded chicken.
4. Boil for 2-3 minutes.
5. Add boiled noodles, remove from fire. Serve.

Chicken Recipes

Chicken in Hot Garlic Sauce

Serves 4 *Picture on page 1*

200 gms chicken breast (boneless)
1 tbsp chopped garlic
2 tsp red chilli paste or 1 tsp red chilli powder
3 tbsp tomato ketchup
¾ tsp salt, or to taste
¼ tsp ajinomoto (optional)
2 cups chicken stock (page 31) or water
1½ tbsp cornflour
4 tbsp oil
1 tbsp vinegar, 2 tsp soya sauce, 1 tsp red chilli sauce
1 tbsp capsicum - cut into tiny cubes (diced)
1 tbsp onions - finely chopped
2 tsp spring onions - finely chopped

MARINADE
1 egg
¾ tsp salt
¼ tsp ajinomoto (optional)
1 tbsp cornflour
1 tbsp oil

1. Cut the chicken breast into even sized pieces.
2. Marinate the chicken in all the ingredients of the marinade and keep aside.
3. Heat 4 tbsp oil in a wok and stir-fry the chicken for 3-4 minutes. Drain and keep aside.
4. To the oil remaining in the wok, add garlic and chilli paste. When garlic changes colour, add tomato ketchup.
5. Add the capsicum, onion and spring onion. Stir-fry for 1 minute.
6. Add chicken. Stir-fry and add salt, ajinomoto, sugar and stock or water. Boil. Cook on low heat till chicken turns tender.
7. Dissolve cornflour in 2-3 tbsp of water and add to the chicken. Thicken the sauce, stirring continuously. Finish with vinegar, red chilli sauce and soya sauce.
8. Serve hot along with boiled rice or noodles.

Dry Chilli Chicken

Picture on facing page *Serves 6*

500 gms chicken - cut into 2" bite size pieces (if desired it can be boneless)
6-8 green chillies - slit lengthwise
3 tbsp oil
1-2 spring onions - cut into ½" pieces

MARINADE
2 tbsp ginger-garlic paste
3 tbsp soya sauce, 1 tbsp vinegar, 1 tsp red chilli powder
1 tsp sugar, ½ tsp ajinomoto (optional), ½ tsp salt
2 tbsp sherry (optional)

1. Marinate the chicken pieces in the marinade for at least 2 hours.
2. Heat oil. Fry green chillies lightly and remove. Add the marinated chicken pieces along with the marinade. Fry well till it dries up.
3. Add ¼ cup water and cook covered till chicken is soft and dry.
4. Mix in the green chillies and serve sprinkled with spring onions.

Honey Lemon Chicken

Serves 8

1 kg chicken pieces
3 tsp soya sauce, 1 tbsp dry sherry
3-4 tbsp honey, juice of 2 lemons
3 tbsp oil
1 tbsp grated ginger
1 tbsp crushed garlic
¼ tsp salt
1½ cups chicken stock (page 31) or water
1½ tbsp cornflour dissolved in 3 tbsp water
slices of fresh lemon to serve

1. Pierce chicken pieces with a skewer. Combine soya sauce, sherry, lemon juice and honey. Brush over chicken pieces and let it stand for 30 minutes.
2. Heat oil. Add ginger, garlic and salt.
3. Add drained chicken pieces and brown evenly.
4. Add marinade and stock. Simmer covered until tender. Turn chicken pieces twice during cooking. Remove chicken pieces and place on a serving platter.
5. Stir cornflour paste into the sauce and bring to a boil, stirring continuously. Spoon sauce over the chicken pieces. Serve with lemon slices.

Lychee Chicken

Serves 8

1 kg boneless chicken - cut into 1" x ½" pieces
8-10 lychees (fresh or canned)
1 medium sized onion - sliced finely
1 green capsicum - sliced finely
1 red capsicum - sliced finely
oil for frying

BATTER
1 tbsp sesame oil
1 egg - lightly beaten
1 tsp salt
1 tsp sugar
¼ cup cornflour

SAUCE
2 tbsp sugar
3 tbsp tomato ketchup
½ tsp salt, a pinch of pepper powder
1½ tbsp worcestershire sauce
1 tbsp vinegar
1½ tbsp cornflour - dissolved in ½ cup water

1. Cut the chicken meat into ½" thick and 1" long pieces.
2. To prepare the batter, beat sesame seed oil into the lightly beaten egg. Add salt, sugar and cornflour.
3. Add chicken pieces to the batter, stir and marinate for 30 minutes.
4. Heat oil. Fry chicken pieces for 4-5 minutes. Keep aside.
5. Heat 3 tbsp oil in a wok. Stir fry onions and capsicums.
6. Add all the other ingredients of the sauce, except cornflour.
7. Add lychees. Cook until the liquid has reduced a little.
8. Add cornflour paste, stirring continuously. Cook till the sauce turns thick.
9. Add the fried chicken pieces to the sauce. Serve hot.

Chicken Manchurian

Serves 4

½ chicken - cut into 1" square pieces

EGG BATTER

1 egg
1½ tbsp cornflour
1½ tbsp plain flour *(maida)*
salt and pepper to taste

MANCHURIAN SAUCE

2 tbsp oil
2 tbsp crushed ginger
2 tbsp crushed garlic
2 tbsp crushed green chillies
2 tbsp chopped coriander
1 cup chicken stock (page 31)
1 tsp sherry - optional
1 tbsp soya sauce
¼ tsp salt
¼ tsp pepper
¼ tsp sugar
¼ tsp ajinomoto (optional)
2-3 tbsp cornflour dissolved in ¼ cup water

1. Mix all ingredients of the batter.
2. Dip the chicken pieces in the batter, deep fry till golden brown. Keep aside.
3. For the manchurian sauce, heat oil in a wok . Lightly fry garlic and ginger till they just change colour.
4. Add green chillies and coriander leaves. Mix.
5. Reduce heat, add chicken stock, soya sauce, sherry, salt, sugar, pepper and ajinomoto. Cook for 2-3 minutes.
6. Add cornflour mixed with water and give one boil. Add fried chicken and cook for 1-2 minutes. Serve hot.

Sesame Chicken

Serves 4

STUFFING
chicken breasts of 1 chicken - minced finely
1 cucumber
1 tbsp finely chopped spring onions
1 tbsp each of finely chopped ginger and garlic
1 tsp salt
1 tbsp rice wine (optional)
a pinch of ajinomoto (optional)
1 tbsp cornflour

WRAPPERS
3 eggs
3 tbsp flour
½ cup white sesame seeds *(til)*
oil for frying

1. Peel cucumber and cut it lengthwise into half. Scoop out seeds. Cut into 1" pieces. Sprinkle salt and place in a colander (metal strainer with holes) with a plate and a weight on top for about 15 minutes, to extract as much water as possible. Rinse under running water and dry thoroughly.
2. Make a thick paste of the cucumber pieces in a blender.
3. Mince the chicken meat finely.
4. Mix chicken, cucumber paste, ginger, garlic, spring onion, salt, wine, ajinomoto and cornflour. Blend well. Keep aside.
5. Beat 2 eggs lightly and make the thinnest possible omelettes of the size of a saucer. 2 eggs will give 10 wafer thin omelettes.
6. Beat the remaining egg with flour and make a thick coating batter. Use water if necessary.
7. Place a small quantity of the chicken mixture in the centre of each omelette and roll up into parcels, approximately 3/4" thick and 2½" long.
8. Coat the outside of the parcels carefully with the thick batter and sprinkle sesame seeds all over.
9. Heat about ½ cup oil in a wok or a frying pan and fry the parcels gently for 5 minutes turning very carefully till golden brown. Serve hot.

Chicken Capsicum

Serves 4

½ kg chicken - shredded
3 capsicums - shredded
2 tbsp oil
½-1 tsp chilli powder
4 flakes garlic - crushed, 2-3 spring onions - chopped
2 tbsp shredded bamboo shoots, 1 cup chicken stock (page 31)
¼ tsp each of salt, sugar, pepper and ajinomoto (optional)
1 tsp sherry, 3 tsp soya sauce
3 tsp cornflour dissolved in ¼ cup water

1. In a frying pan heat 2 tbsp oil, reduce heat and add chilli powder.
2. Mix in crushed garlic, fry a little and add chicken pieces. Fry to a pale colour.
3. Add chopped spring onions, fry for a minute, add bamboo shoots & fry for 1 minute. Reduce heat.
4. Add chicken stock, salt, sugar, pepper, ajinomoto and soya sauce. Cook for 5 minutes.
5. Mix cornflour with little water, reduce heat and add it to the chicken, stirring continuously.
6. Add capsicum. Further cook for 3-4 minutes. Serve hot.

Chicken & Vegetable Satay

Serves 6

225 gms chicken breast, skin removed - cut in 3/4" cubes
1 tbsp soya sauce
1 medium onion - quartered
½ red capsicum - cut into 3/4" cubes, 8 button mushrooms
4 long bamboo satay sticks, soaked in water to prevent burning
¼ cup orange juice

1. Combine chicken and vegetables with soya sauce and let it marinate for 15 minutes. Thread chicken, onion, red capsicum and mushrooms on to satay sticks. Place on a sheet of foil and brush with orange juice.
2. Broil in an oven under medium heat until chicken is done. Baste with orange juice frequently to prevent drying out. Serve with brown rice.

Spicy Honey Chicken

Picture on facing page **_Serves 4_**

250 gm chicken breast boneless
½ cup cornflour - approx.
2-3 dry, red chillies - broken into bits
2 tsp garlic paste
2 tbsp spring onions - white part finely chopped and greens cut into 1" pieces
2½ tbsp tomato ketchup
1½-2 tbsp soya sauce
2 tsp honey
oil for frying

MARINADE
2 eggs
½ tsp salt
½ tsp ajinomoto (optional)
1 tbsp cornflour
1 tbsp oil

1. Cut the chicken breast into even slices.
2. Mix all the ingredients of the marinade and marinate the chicken & keep aside for 1 hour.
3. Coat the marinated chicken with dry cornflour. See to it that each piece is coated.
4. Deep fry the chicken till crisp and golden brown. Drain and keep aside.
5. Heat 2 tbsp oil in a wok.
6. Reduce heat. Add dry, red chillies and stir. Add garlic paste. Stir for a few seconds.
7. Add finely chopped white part of spring onions, tomato ketchup, soya sauce & honey. Saute for a few seconds.
8. Add the crispy fried chicken and stir-fry ensuring that each piece is coated with the sauce. Mix in the greens of spring onions. Serve hot.

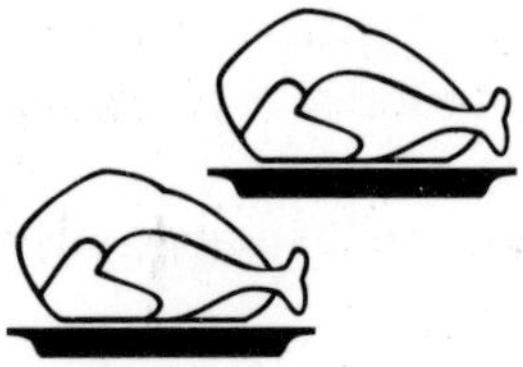

Chicken HongKong

Serves 4

½ chicken - cut into bite size (1½ - 2") pieces
3 tbsp shelled walnuts
2-3 spring onions - finely sliced diagonally
3 tbsp oil
3 dry, red chillies - broken into bits
½ tsp chilli powder
1" piece ginger - sliced
½ cup chicken stock (page 31)
2 tsp cornflour dissolved in ¼ cup water

MARINADE

1 tbsp soya sauce
2 tsp sherry - optional
1 tsp cornflour
salt to taste
¼ tsp sugar
a pinch of ajinomoto (optional)

1. Cut the chicken cut into 1½" - 2" square pieces.
2. In a bowl mix together all the ingredients of the marinade - soya sauce, sherry, cornflour, salt, sugar and ajinomoto. Mix in the chicken pieces. Leave to marinate for at least 1 hour or more.
3. In a wok heat 3 tbsp oil. Fry walnuts to golden brown. Remove from oil and keep aside.
4. To the remaining oil, add broken dried, red chillies. Reduce heat and add chilli powder.
5. Add ginger. Stir-fry for 2-3 minutes.
6. Add the marinated chicken pieces. Fry till oil separates.
7. Add the chicken stock and further cook for 5 minutes.
8. Reduce heat and add cornflour paste to the chicken, stirring continuously. Cook for 3-5 minutes till the sauce turns thick.
9. Garnish with finely sliced spring onions and fried walnuts.

Chicken Sweet & Sour

Serves 4

200 gms chicken leg boneless
1½ tbsp tomato ketchup
1 tbsp malt vinegar
1 tbsp sugar
¼ tsp ajinomoto (optional)
1/3 cup chicken stock (page 31)
oil for frying
1 tbsp diced (finely cut) capsicum
1 tbsp carrots - cut into dices and dipped in boiling water for a few seconds
1 tbsp onions - chopped
1 tbsp cornflour

BATTER
2 eggs
2 tbsp plain flour (maida)
1 tbsp cornflour

1. Cut the chicken into even sized (1" square) pieces.
2. Mix eggs, plain flour and cornflour to make a thick, smooth batter. Marinate the chicken in this batter and keep aside for 15-20 minutes.
3. Heat oil and deep-fry the chicken pieces individually till cooked & golden brown in colour. Keep aside.
4. In a wok add stock and bring the stock to a boil.
5. Add tomato ketchup, ajinomoto and sugar. Boil for 1 minute.
6. Dissolve the cornflour in 2 tbsp water and add to the stock, stirring continuously till the sauce thickens.
7. Add the vegetables and chicken. Cook for 1 minute.
8. Add malt vinegar and remove from fire. Serve hot.

Pork & Lamb

Szechwan Pork

Serves 6-8

1 kg pork ribs - cut into 1 inch squares
2 tsp chopped ginger
3 tbsp brown sugar
3 tbsp soya sauce
2 tbsp sherry
½ tsp five spice powder (recipe given below)
1 cup oil

SZECHWAN SAUCE

3 tbsp oil
2-3 dry, red chillies - broken into bits
3 red or green capsicums - chopped into ½" pieces
2 tsp chopped garlic
2 tsp chopped ginger
2 spring onions - chopped
2 tbsp sugar
2 tbsp sherry
5 tbsp tomato ketchup
5 tbsp vinegar

5 SPICE POWDER

(Grind together to a fine powder in equal quantities, store the excess)
peppercorns
cinnamon
cloves
fennel
star anise

1. Place ribs in a pan, add water, cover and bring to a boil. Cook for 30 minutes. Drain well.
2. Combine ginger, sugar, soya sauce, sherry and five spice powder. Add ribs and marinate for 2 hours.
3. Heat oil. Deep fry ribs until golden. Drain well. Keep aside.
4. To prepare the sauce heat oil in a pan. Add the broken red chillies. Add capsicum, ginger, garlic and onion. Fry for 1-2 minutes.
5. Add sherry, sugar, ketchup and vinegar. Simmer for 5 minutes.
6. Add ribs, stirring to coat. Serve hot.

Sweet & Sour Pork

Serves 4-6

250 gms pork - cut into 1" cubes
½ cup carrots - cut into tiny cubes
½ cup onion - cut into tiny cubes
½ cup cucumber - cut into tiny cubes
2 flakes garlic - minced

MARINADE
1 tsp sherry
½ tsp salt
¼ tsp pepper

BATTER
1 egg - beaten
1 tbsp plain flour *(maida)*
2 tbsp cornflour

SAUCE
3 tbsp tomato ketchup
1 tsp soya sauce, 3 tbsp vinegar
3 tbsp sugar
½ cup water
1 tbsp cornflour

1. Mix pork cubes with the ingredients of the marinade.
2. Mix all ingredients of the batter together. Coat pork with the batter.
3. Heat oil and drop in pork cubes one by one. Deep fry until well done, over medium heat. Drain.
4. Fry carrots, onion and cucumber for 1 minute & drain. Keep aside.
5. Mix all ingredients of the sauce together.
6. Heat 4 tbsp oil, fry 2 flakes of minced garlic till light brown.
7. Add the ingredients of the sauce mixed together, stirring continuously.
8. Simmer on low flame until thickened.
9. Add pork and vegetables and mix well. Serve hot.

Pork or Mince Meat Balls

Serves 6

BALLS

1½ cups ground or finely chopped pork or lamb
1 spring onion - finely chopped
2 thin slices ginger - finely chopped
2 flakes garlic - crushed and chopped
½ tsp salt
½ tsp sugar
2-3 tbsp soya sauce
2 tsp sesame oil
2 tbsp rice wine
¼ tsp pepper
½ tsp ajinomoto (optional)
¼ cup cornflour
¼ cup plain flour *(maida)*
1-2 green chillies - finely chopped

OTHER INGREDIENTS

2 eggs - lightly beaten
½ cup cornflour
oil for frying

1. Thoroughly mix all ingredients listed in the ingredients for the balls.
2. Shape this mixture into small balls.
3. Dip in lightly beaten eggs and roll in cornflour to coat. Shake off excess.
4. Heat oil in a wok and fry the meat balls until golden brown all over.
5. Serve hot along with chilli sauce.

Fried Spare Ribs/Lamb Chops

Serves 4

8 pork spare ribs or lamb chops
2-3 spring onions - chopped
5 thin slices fresh ginger - chopped
2-3 flakes garlic - chopped
oil for frying

SAUCE

1 spring onion - shredded
2 capsicums - shredded
2 tbsp oil
1 tbsp sesame oil
a pinch of sugar
¼ cup soya sauce
1 tsp salt
a pinch ajinomoto (optional)

1. Cut the spare ribs or chops into even sized pieces (1½" squares).
2. Chop spring onions, ginger and garlic. Place in a bowl with spare ribs or chops and mix well. Leave to stand for a short while.
3. Take a large saucepan with water to boil. Add spare ribs or chops and seasonings and simmer for 10-15 minutes.
4. Remove spare ribs or chops and drain well.
5. Heat oil in a wok and fry spare ribs or chops until golden brown.
6. Heat 2 tbsp oil and fry the shredded spring onions and capsicum.
7. Add soya sauce, sesame oil, ajinomoto, salt and sugar. Stir well.
8. Add the spare ribs or chops and coat with the sauce. Cook for 5-10 minutes to reduce and thicken sauce. Serve hot.

Braised Lamb in 5 Spice Powder

Serves 4

½ kg boneless lamb - cut into 1" square pieces
1 cup water
4 tbsp soya sauce
2 tbsp sherry
1 tbsp sliced or shredded ginger
1 tbsp honey
1 tbsp oil
1 tbsp 5 spice powder (recipe given below)

5 SPICE POWDER
(Grind together to a fine powder in equal quantities and store the excess)
peppercorns
cinnamon
cloves
fennel
star anise

1. In a cooker, mix water, soya sauce, sherry and ginger.
2. Bring to a boil and add the meat pieces. Cover and cook over low heat till the meat is tender.
3. Add honey and oil. Further cook over low heat for 15-20 minutes.
4. Add 1 tbsp five spice powder.
5. Garnish with sliced spring onions.
6. Serve hot with noodles or steamed rice.

Sea Food

Crispy Fried Fish

Serves 2

1 whole pomfret
1 tsp salt
3 tbsp rice wine
a pinch of ajinomoto (optional)
3 tbsp cornflour
oil for frying
1½ tbsp finely chopped spring onions

SAUCE

¼ cup oil
1½ tsp finely chopped ginger
1½ tbsp sugar
¼ tsp pepper
3 tbsp vinegar
1/3 cup tomato ketchup

1. Make slanting slashes all down both sides of fish about 3/4" apart. Repeat in opposite direction.
2. Mix salt, rice wine and 1½ tbsp cornflour in a shallow dish, large enough to contain the fish. Roll fish in this mixture turning the sides. Leave to stand for 15 minutes.
3. Heat about ½ cup oil over high heat. Reduce heat. Add fish and fry over moderate heat. Remove and place in a dish.
4. To prepare the sauce, in a saucepan heat ¼ cup fresh oil and stir fry finely chopped spring onions and ginger for a few seconds.
5. Add sugar, vinegar, pepper and ketchup and cook to reduce and thicken.
6. Pour the sauce over the cooked fish.

Jumbo Prawns with Lemon Sauce

Serves 4

12 jumbo prawns - shelled & deveined
1 lemon - cut into thin slices
oil for frying

MARINADE

1 egg - lightly beaten
1 tsp salt, ½-1 tsp sugar
½ tsp ajinomoto (optional)
1 tsp sesame seed oil
¼ tsp pepper powder
¼ cup cornflour

SAUCE

1 medium sized onion
3 tbsp oil
1 tsp salt
2 tbsp lemon juice
2½ tbsp sugar
1½ tbsp cornflour

1. Beat egg lightly with salt, sugar, ajinomoto, sesame seed oil, pepper and cornflour.
2. Add prawns to this mixture, stir and leave to marinate for 30 minutes.
3. Peel and make the onion into two halves. Cut thin semi circles to get wafer thin slices of onion.
4. To prepare the sauce, heat 3 tbsp oil in a wok and stir fry the onion slices. Add lemon juice, salt and sugar. Cook over high heat to reduce a little.
5. Mix cornflour with very little water and stir into the sauce to thicken. Keep sauce aside.
6. Heat plenty of oil in wok. Drain off excess marinade from the prawns and fry them to golden brown.
7. Drain well and place on paper towel.
8. Slice lemon very thinly into rounds. Add these to the piping hot sauce with the prawns. Stir to mix well and serve at once.

Steamed Fish with Garlic & Ginger

Serves 6

3/4 kg cleaned fish fillet (boneless)
1 tbsp finely chopped fresh ginger
1 tbsp finely chopped garlic
3 tbsp oil
2 spring onions - finely chopped

SAUCE
3 tbsp chicken stock (page 31)
1½ tbsp soya sauce
3 tbsp sesame seed oil/refined oil
¼ tsp pepper powder, 1½ tbsp rice wine
1 tbsp chilli garlic sauce, ¼ tsp ajinomoto (optional)
1 tbsp cornflour mixed with 2 tbsp water

1. Steam cleaned fish pieces with garlic, ginger and oil for 3-4 minutes.
2. Mix all the ingredients of the sauce in a small saucepan & stir over high heat. Bring to a boil.
3. Add cornflour, stirring continuously till the sauce turns thick.
4. Transfer the cooked fish to a heated serving platter.
5. Pour the sauce all over.
6. Sprinkle finely chopped spring onions.

Honeyed Shrimps

Serves 4

750 gm shrimps - peeled with tail intact
3 tbsp oil
1 clove garlic - crushed
1" piece ginger - finely chopped
¼ cup honey
2 tsp soya sauce
a few sesame seeds *(til)*

1. Heat oil in a wok. Add garlic and ginger and stir-fry for 30 seconds.
2. Add shrimp in two batches and stir-fry until pink. Remove the first batch before cooking the second.
3. Add honey & soya sauce and toss quickly. Serve sprinkled with sesame seeds.

Prawns in Garlic Sauce

Picture on facing page **Serves 6**

12 prawns - shelled & deveined
oil for frying

MARINADE
1 egg - lightly beaten
1 tsp salt, ½-1 tsp sugar
¼ tsp ajinomoto (optional)
1 tsp oil
¼ tsp pepper powder
¼ cup cornflour

SAUCE
2 tbsp garlic paste
2 tbsp oil
4 tbsp tomato ketchup, 2-3 tsp soya sauce
1¼ cups water
½ tsp white pepper, 3/4 tsp salt
2 tbsp cornflour mixed with ½ cup water
a pinch of sugar
¼ tsp ajinomoto (optional)

1. Beat egg lightly with salt, sugar, ajinomoto, sesame seed oil, pepper and cornflour.
2. Add prawns to this mixture, stir and leave to marinate for 30 minutes.
3. Heat plenty of oil in wok. Drain off excess marinade from the prawns and fry them to golden brown.
4. Drain well and place on paper towel.
5. To prepare the sauce, heat oil and fry the garlic on low heat till it starts to change it's colour.
6. Add tomato ketchup, pepper, salt and soya sauce. Cook for 1 minute.
7. Add sugar and ajinomoto.
8. Add water. Bring to a boil and simmer for 2 minutes.
9. Add cornflour paste, stirring all the time, until the sauce thickens. Remove from heat.
10. Add the fried prawns and heat through. Serve hot.

Szechwan Mandarin Fish

Serves 2

½ kg medium sized pomfret

EGG BATTER
1 egg
¼ tsp salt
¼ tsp pepper
¼ tsp ajinomoto (optional)
1½ tbsp flour
1½ tbsp cornflour

SAUCE
1 tbsp oil
2 broken, dried chillies
½ - 1 tsp chilli powder
4 flakes garlic - crushed
3 tbsp vinegar
2 tbsp sugar
2 tsp soya sauce
2 tsp tomato ketchup
¼ tsp salt
¼ tsp pepper
¼ tsp ajinomoto (optional)
1 tsp sherry or rice wine
3/4 cup chicken stock (page 31)
3 tsp cornflour dissolved in ¼ cup water
a few carrot flowers, onion rings and cucumber slices - to garnish

1. Make egg batter by mixing egg, flour, cornflour and seasonings.
2. Keep the fish full. Remove the eggs. Make a slit near the gills and lower mouth and clean the fish.
3. Make deep cuts on both sides of the fish. Salt it.
4. Add it to the egg batter. Leave for 15-20 minutes.
5. In a wok heat oil. Reduce heat and add all the ingredients of the sauce, except cornflour. Cook for 5 minutes on low flame.
6. Add cornflour paste. Cook for 3-4 minutes, stirring continuously.
7. Before serving fry the fish to a golden brown colour over medium heat.
8. Place it in a flat serving dish. Pour the sauce over it and garnish with carrot flowers, onion rings and cucumber slices.

Stir Fried Shrimps

Serves 4

½ kg shrimps - heads removed, shelled, deveined, cleaned and dried
egg white
a pinch of ajinomoto (optional)
1 tsp salt, 1 tbsp cornflour, 2½ tbsp rice wine
1/3 cup fresh or frozen peas

SAUCE
3 tbsp oil
a pinch of ajinomoto (optional), a pinch of salt, 1½ tbsp rice wine

1. Beat egg white adding ajinomoto, salt, cornflour and rice wine. Add shrimp, stir and leave to marinate.
2. Boil peas in water to which a little sugar and salt is added. Drain.
3. Heat oil in a wok. Add shrimps and peas, fry for 1 minute. Drain and set aside.
4. Heat 3 tbsp of oil with a pinch of salt and ajinomoto and 1½ tbsp rice wine. Return the shrimp and peas to the wok and stir fry for 2 minutes.
5. Serve on a bed of lettuce or cabbage leaves.

Shrimp Chow Mein

Serves 4

450 gm shrimp - peeled
10 Chinese mushrooms - soaked in warm water for 20 minutes
3 tbsp oil
2 stalks celery - sliced
100 gm bamboo shoots - sliced
200 gm bean sprouts - washed
200 gm water chestnuts - drained and sliced
½ cup chicken stock (page 31), 1 tbsp dry sherry
1 tbsp soya sauce

1. Drain mushrooms, squeeze dry and discard stalks. Slice caps into strips.
2. Heat oil in a wok. Add celery, bamboo shoots, mushrooms, bean sprouts and water chestnuts. Stir-fry about 2 minutes until vegetables are tender but crisp.
3. Pour in stock and sherry. Increase heat to high and bring to a boil. Reduce heat.
4. Stir in soya sauce and shrimps. Cover and cook for 3 minutes. Remove from heat and serve immediately.

Fish in Garlic Sauce

Serves 6

250 gms fish - cut into 1" square pieces
oil for frying
2 tbsp oil
1 tbsp chopped garlic
1 tsp chopped ginger
2-3 dry, broken red chillies
½ cup fresh tomato puree - prepared by grinding tomatoes in a mixer
½ cup tomato ketchup
1 cup chicken stock (page 31)
2 tsp soya sauce
1 tsp sherry
¼ tsp salt
¼ tsp sugar
¼ tsp ajinomoto (optional)
3 tsp cornflour - dissolved in ¼ cup water

EGG BATTER
1 egg
1½ tbsp flour
1½ tbsp cornflour
½ cup water
salt - to taste

1. Prepare egg batter by mixing all the ingredients of the batter together to a dropping consistency.
2. In a wok heat oil. Dip fish in egg batter and deep fry till golden brown. Keep aside.
3. In a frying pan heat 2 tbsp oil. Reduce heat. Add dried red chillies.
4. Add garlic and ginger. Fry for a minute. Add fresh tomato puree. Stir fry till dry.
5. Add tomato ketchup. Mix. Add stock. Bring to a boil and cook for 2-3 minutes.
6. Add soya sauce, sherry, salt, ajinomoto and sugar.
7. Mix cornflour in water and add to the sauce, stirring continuously. Bring to a boil.
8. Add fish, cook for 2-3 minutes. Garnish with spring onions. Serve hot.

Vegetable Dishes

Honey Chilli Veggies on Rice

Picture on cover **Serves 4**

1 small carrot - parboiled and cut into round slices
¼ of a small cauliflower or broccoli - cut into small, flat florets and parboiled
1 small onion - cut into 4 pieces and separated
4-5 mushrooms
4-6 baby corns (optional)
1 capsicum - cut into ½" cubes
1 tbsp soya sauce, 2 tsp chilli sauce, 1½ tbsp tomato sauce
1-1¼ tbsp honey, ½ tbsp vinegar
¼ tsp freshly ground pepper, 1 tsp salt, or to taste, a pinch ajinomoto (optional)
3 tbsp cornflour mixed with ¼ cup water
2-3 tbsp oil
3-4 dried, red chillies - broken into small pieces
8-10 flakes garlic - crushed
1 tbsp ginger - grated

TO SERVE
4 cups boiled rice

1. To parboil vegetables, boil 4 cups water with 1 tsp salt. Peel the carrot and drop the whole carrot and cauliflower florets in boiling water. Let them boil for 2-3 minutes. Remove from water. Cut carrots into ¼" thick round slices.
2. Cut capsicum into ½" pieces. Trim mushrooms and baby corns, keeping them whole. Cut onion into fours and separate the slices.
3. Dissolve cornflour in ¼ cup water and keep aside.
4. Heat oil in a kadhai. Reduce heat and add broken red chillies and half the garlic. Add ginger.
5. Stir and add baby corns, carrots, cauliflower, onion and mushrooms. Stir for 4-5 minutes. Add capsicum. Add salt and pepper. Mix and remove these stir-fried vegetables from the kadhai.
6. Heat 1 tbsp oil in the same kadhai, add the left over garlic, reduce heat. Add chilli sauce, tomato sauce, soya sauce, honey and vinegar. Stir for 2 minutes. Pour 2 cups of water and bring to a boil. Lower heat and simmer for 2 minutes.
7. Add the dissolved cornflour and cook till the sauce turns thick.
8. Spread the warm rice in a serving plate. Pour the hot sauce over the rice. Cover it with hot stir-fried vegetables and serve immediately.

Steamed Spinach in Hot Garlic Sauce

Serves 4

250 gm spinach

GARLIC SAUCE
2 tsp garlic paste
2-3 dried red chillies - broken into bits
2 tsp soya sauce
2 tbsp tomato ketchup
2 tsp vinegar
½ tsp pepper
¼ tsp sugar
1½ tbsp cornflour dissolved in 1 cup water
2 tbsp oil

1. Wash spinach. Discard stems, keeping the leaves whole.
2. Steam the spinach leaves by keeping in a metal strainer or a colander over a pan of boiling water for 5 minutes.
3. Keep the steamed spinach aside.
4. Heat oil. Add garlic paste. Reduce heat. Fry till it starts to change colour.
5. Add the red chilli bits. Stir for a few seconds.
6. Add soya sauce and tomato ketchup. Mix for a few seconds.
7. Add vinegar.
8. Add the cornflour paste, stirring continuously. Add salt, pepper and sugar. Cook till thick. Keep aside.
9. At serving time, mix in the steamed spinach. Serve with steamed rice.

Cauliflower with fried Noodles

Serves 6

1 medium cauliflower
1½ cups boiled noodles
5 tbsp oil
2 tsp finely grated ginger
3-4 green chillies - slit lengthwise
¼ tsp ajinomoto (optional)
¼ tsp salt and pepper, or to taste
3-4 flakes garlic - crushed
1 tbsp soya sauce
spring onion greens or slit green chillies - to garnish

MIX TOGETHER FOR THE SAUCE
3/4 cup water
2 level tbsp cornflour
1 tbsp soya sauce
2½ - 3 tbsp tomato ketchup
½ tsp crushed red chilli powder
1 tbsp vinegar
salt and pepper to taste

1. Cut cauliflower into medium sized florets. Boil in salted water for 1-2 minutes till just tender. Do not cook for too long. Strain.
2. Heat 3 tbsp oil in a wok. Add grated ginger and green chillies. Stir till ginger changes colour.
3. Add cauliflower. Add ajinomoto and stir fry till cauliflower turns light brown.
4. Shift the cauliflower to the sides of the wok, leaving the centre empty. Add all the ingredients mixed together for the sauce in the centre and give one boil. Mix all the ingredients to blend well. Remove from wok and keep aside.
5. Heat 2 tbsp oil in a clean wok. Reduce heat. Add garlic. When garlic turns light brown, add soya sauce. Stir well. Add boiled noodles and fry for 1-2 minutes till they turn brown. Add a little salt and pepper to taste.
6. Remove from wok and spread on a serving platter.
7. Pour the hot cauliflower in sauce over the fried noodles. Garnish with spring onion greens or slit green chillies.
8. Sprinkle crushed red chilli powder. Serve hot.

Cauliflower Manchurian

Serves 4

MANCHURIAN BALLS
2 tsp cornflour
2 tsp plain flour *(maida)*
1½ cups grated cauliflower
1 tsp red chilli paste
½ tsp baking powder
salt to taste
¼ cup milk
2 tbsp bread crumbs

MANCHURIAN SAUCE
1½ tbsp oil
1 tsp garlic paste
2 green chillies
2 tsp soya sauce
2 tsp vinegar
1½ tbsp tomato ketchup
½ tsp salt
1½ cups water
2 tbsp cornflour dissolved in ½ cup water
green leaves of 2 spring onions - chopped

1. Mix plain flour, cornflour, baking powder, red chilli paste and salt to taste. Make a thick batter with milk.
2. Add cauliflower and mix well. Shape into flat balls.
3. Roll in bread crumbs and deep fry. Keep aside.
4. To prepare the sauce, heat 2 tbsp oil. Stir fry garlic and green chillies for ½ minute on low flame.
5. Add soya sauce, tomato ketchup and vinegar. Cook for ½ minute.
6. Add water. Boil.
7. Add cornflour paste, stirring continuously. Cook till the sauce thickens. Add spring onion greens.
8. To serve, boil the sauce. Add the balls, keep on low flame for ½ minute. Serve hot.

Stir fried Red & Green Cabbage

Picture on facing page *Serves 4*

1 small green cabbage - shredded
½ of a small red cabbage - shredded
3-4 green chillies - shredded
1 capsicum - shredded (optional)
3 tbsp oil
½ tsp ajinomoto (optional)
½ tsp salt, ½ tsp pepper, or to taste
¼ tsp crushed red chillies

MIX TOGETHER IN A CUP
½ cup water
1½ tbsp cornflour
1½ - 2 tbsp soya sauce
2½ - 3 tbsp tomato ketchup
2 tbsp vinegar

1. Shred cabbage and capsicum into thin strips.
2. Heat oil. Add cabbage, capsicum and green chillies. Stir fry for 1-2 minutes.
3. Add salt, pepper and ajinomoto.
4. Add all the ingredients which have been mixed together in a cup. Stir fry on low heat for 2-3 minutes till the vegetable is almost dry, but not completely dry.
5. Serve hot, sprinkled with crushed red chillies.

The Chinese Sizzler

Hot ginger or garlic sauce is poured over stir fried vegetables placed on a hot iron plate. Noodle cutlets and french fries accompany the vegetables.

Serves 4

NOODLE CUTLETS
3 boiled potatoes - grated
1 carrot - cut into tiny cubes
1 capsicum - cut into tiny cubes
1 onion - chopped finely
1 tsp salt, ½ tsp red chilli powder
1 tsp soya sauce, 2 tbsp oil
6 tbsp bread crumbs

COATING
2 tbsp plain flour *(maida)* mixed with ¼ cup water
1 cup boiled noodles

1. Heat oil. Stir fry onion for ½ minute. Add carrot and capsicum. Stir fry for 1 minute.
2. Add potatoes, soya sauce, salt and chilli powder. Mix well.
3. Remove from fire. Add bread crumbs. Mix well and shape into oval balls. Flatten them slightly.
4. Dip in a thin batter prepared by mixing 2 tbsp plain flour with ¼ cup water.
4. Cover with boiled noodles. Deep fry to a golden brown colour. Keep the noodle cutlets aside.

GINGER SAUCE
2" piece ginger, 2 dry, red chillies
2 tbsp oil
1 tsp soya sauce , 2 tbsp tomato ketchup
1 tbsp vinegar
¼ tsp ajinomoto (optional), ½ tsp each of salt and pepper, or to taste
1 cup water
1½ tbsp cornflour dissolved in ½ cup water

1. Grind red chillies with ginger to a paste.
2. Heat oil. Stir fry paste on low flame for 1 minute.
3. Add soya sauce, tomato ketchup, vinegar, ajinomoto, salt and pepper. Cook for 1 minute.
4. Add water. Boil. Add cornflour paste, stirring continuously. Cook till thick.

STIR FRIED VEGETABLES

¼ of a small cauliflower, parboiled - cut into florets
5-6 parboiled french beans - cut into 1" long pieces
2 cabbage leaves - torn into big pieces
1 carrot - parboiled, cut into leaves and flowers
1 onion - cut into fours and separated
salt and pepper to taste
¼ tsp ajinomoto (optional)
a pinch of sugar
2 tbsp oil

1. Heat oil. Add onions.
2. Stir fry for 1 minute. Add cauliflower.
3. Stir fry for 2 minutes. Add all other vegetables, salt, pepper, ajinomoto & sugar. Stir fry for a few seconds. Remove from fire.

TO SERVE

a few cabbage leaves
50 gm chilled butter - cut into ¼" cubes
juice of 1 lemon
a few potato fingers

1. To serve, remove the iron plate from the wooden stand. Heat the iron plate on high flame, till very hot. Place it back on the wooden stand.
2. Place 2 halves of a cabbage leaf on a hot iron plate fitted on a wooden stand. Push a few tiny cubes of ice cold butter sprinkled with lemon juice under the leaves.
3. Arrange the noodle cutlets and stir fried vegetables on the cabbage leaves.
4. Pour the prepared hot sauce over it.
5. Fried potato fingers may accompany the sizzler.

Garlic Cauliflower

Serves 4

BATTER

1 medium cauliflower - cut into big florets
2 tbsp plain flour (maida)
2 tbsp cornflour
a pinch of soda-bicarb
¼ tsp each of salt, pepper
¼ tsp ajinomoto (optional)

GARLIC SAUCE

1 pod of garlic - crushed and chopped
1 tbsp finely chopped green chillies
¼ cup tomato ketchup
2 tomatoes - ground to a puree
4 tbsp water (approx.)
½ tsp each of salt and pepper
½ tsp sugar
1 cup water
2 tbsp cornflour dissolved in ¼ cup water
2 tbsp oil

1. Mix plain flour, cornflour, salt, pepper and ajinomoto. Add water to make a thick batter of coating consistency.
2. Dip cauliflower in batter and deep fry. Keep aside
3. Heat 2 tbsp oil. Add garlic and green chillies. Cook for ½ minute. Add tomato puree. Cook till tomatoes turn dry.
4. Add tomato ketchup.
5. Add salt, pepper, sugar and 1 cup water. Boil.
6. Add cornflour paste. Stir till thick. Keep the sauce aside.
7. Add the fried cauliflower pieces to the sauce at the time of serving.

Szechwan Vegetables with Nuts

Serves 4

1/3 cup cashewnuts or almonds or walnuts
4 tbsp oil
1 tsp red chilli powder, 3-4 flakes garlic - crushed
2-3 spring onions
2-3 pieces of bamboo shoots
7-8 mushrooms
50 gm or ½ cup boiled and sliced lotus stem
1/3 of a medium cucumber
50 gm cabbage
2 capsicums
1 cup water or vegetable stock (page 31)
¼ tsp each of salt, sugar, pepper
¼ tsp ajinomoto (optional)
3 tsp cornflour
3 tsp soya sauce
1 tsp sherry - optional

1. Slice the vegetables or cut them into square pieces.
2. In a frying pan heat oil. Reduce heat and fry the nuts to golden brown.
3. Remove nuts from oil and keep aside for sprinkling on the top.
4. Add chilli powder to the oil remaining in the pan.
5. Reduce heat and add garlic. Fry for 1 minute on low flame.
6. Stir fry in sequence - onions, bamboo shoots, mushroom, lotus stem, cucumber cabbage and capsicum. Stir fry each vegetable for a few seconds before adding the next vegetable.
7. Reduce heat and add soya sauce, sherry, salt, sugar, pepper and ajinomoto.
8. Cook for 2-3 minutes. Add water. Boil.
9. Mix cornflour with a little water and add to the vegetables.
10. Cook till thick. Garnish with fried nuts.

Vegetable Chow Chow with Mushrooms

Serves 4

3 tbsp oil
4 spring onions - cut into fours
8 mushrooms - sliced
½ cup medium florets of broccoli - parboiled
2 capsicums - cut into ½" pieces
8-10 french beans - parboiled - cut into 1" long pieces
100 gm mushrooms - sliced thickly
¼ tsp ajinomoto (optional)
1 tsp white pepper
salt to taste
1 tsp sugar
½ cup water
1 tbsp soya sauce
½ tbsp vinegar
1 tbsp cornflour mixed with ¼ cup water

1. Boil water with some salt in a pan. Add beans and broccoli florets to the boiling water. Let the boil come again. Drain and keep aside in a strainer.
2. Heat oil. Add onions and mushrooms & stir fry over a high flame for 2 minutes.
3. Add capsicums & stir fry for 1 minute.
4. Add beans and broccoli, ajinomoto, pepper, sugar & salt.
5. Stir fry over high flame for 2 minutes.
6. Add water, soya sauce, chilli sauce & vinegar. Boil.
7. Add cornflour paste, stir briskly for 1 minute. Remove from fire.
8. Serve with boiled rice.

Sweet & Sour Vegetables

Serves 4

TOMATO STOCK
1 onion - chopped
2 big tomatoes - chopped
4-5 flakes garlic - crushed
½" piece ginger
1½ cups water

OTHER INGREDIENTS
1 carrot - parboiled
10 french beans - parboiled
4-5 medium florets of cauliflower - parboiled
¼ of a small cucumber
1 small capsicum - cut into 1" pieces
2 small onions - cut into four pieces
½ tsp white pepper, ¼ tsp ajinomoto (optional)
¼ cup tomato ketchup, 2 - 3 tbsp vinegar
2 tsp sugar, 2 tsp soya sauce
2 tbsp cornflour
3 tbsp oil

1. Pressure cook all ingredients for the tomato stock together to give 2-3 whistles.
2. Remove from fire after the pressure drops down. Strain.
3. Keep the tomato stock aside.
4. Scrape carrot, string french beans.
5. Boil 2-3 cups water with 1 tsp salt. Drop whole carrot, whole french beans & cauliflower florets in the boiling water for one minute. Strain. Cool.
6. Cut beans and carrots diagonally, beans into 1" long pieces and carrots into ¼" thick round slices. Keep aside.
7. Heat 3 tbsp oil. Stir fry onions and cauliflower for 2 minutes.
8. Add all other vegetables.
9. Add salt, pepper & ajinomoto.
10. Stir fry vegetables for 2 minutes.
11. Add the prepared tomato stock.
12. Add tomato ketchup, vinegar, sugar & soya sauce. Boil.
13. Add cornflour mixed with ½ cup water, stirring continuously.
14. Simmer for 2 minutes till thick and the vegetables are cooked. Serve hot with fried rice or noodles.

Baby Corns in Ginger Sauce

Serves 4

2-3 baby corns - sliced into 1" pieces
3 tbsp oil
¼ tsp ajinomoto (optional)
1 tbsp ginger paste
3/4 tsp each of salt & pepper
2 tsp soya sauce
2 tbsp tomato ketchup
½ tsp sugar
1 tbsp cornflour dissolved in 1 cup water
2-3 spring onion greens - cut into 1" pieces

1. Heat 2 tbsp oil in a wok. Add baby corns.
2. Add ¼ tsp salt and ajinomoto.
3. Stir fry for 2-3 minutes till cooked. Remove from wok and keep aside.
4. Heat 1 tbsp more of oil. Add ginger paste. Cook on low flame for ½ minute.
5. Add the spring onion greens.
6. Add ½ tsp each of salt & pepper. Stir fry for a few seconds.
7. Add soya sauce, tomato ketchup and sugar. Cook for ½ minute.
8. Add the stir fried baby corns. Stir to mix well.
9. Add the cornflour paste, stirring continuously. Cook till the sauce turns thick and it coats the baby corns.

Cantonese Vegetables

Serves 8

½ cabbage - cut into big chunks
2 medium sized carrots - parboiled & cut into thick rounds
2 medium sized onions - cut into fours
1 capsicum - cut into 8 pieces
1 small cucumber - cut into rounds
2 cups water
2 tbsp soya sauce
1 tbsp chilli sauce
1 tbsp vinegar
1 tsp pepper
salt to taste
¼ tsp ajinomoto (optional)
1 tsp sugar
2 - 3 tbsp cornflour dissolved in water

1. Wash and cut vegetables into big pieces.
2 Stir fry each vegetable separately in little oil.
3. Do not over fry. The colour of the vegetables should not change.
4. Take out the vegetables into a serving dish.
5. Heat 1 tbsp oil. Add soya sauce, chilli sauce, vinegar, salt, pepper, ajinomoto and sugar. Stir on low heat for a few seconds.
6. Add water. Boil.
7. Add cornflour paste, stirring continuously. Remove from fire when thick.
8. Add the vegetables to the sauce and serve hot.

Vegetable Manchurian

Picture on facing page **Serves 4-6**

MANCHURIAN BALLS
1 cup grated cauliflower
¼ cup grated cabbage
¼ cup grated carrots
2 finely chopped green chillies
1 tbsp cornflour, 1 tbsp plain flour *(maida)*
1 bread slice - dipped in water and squeezed
¼ tsp ajinomoto (optional)
salt and pepper to taste
2-3 tbsp milk, oil for frying

MANCHURIAN SAUCE
2 tbsp oil
1" piece ginger - crushed to a paste, 5-6 flakes garlic - crushed - optional
2 green chillies - chopped, ½ onion - finely chopped
1-2 tsp soya sauce, 1½ tbsp tomato ketchup, 2 tsp vinegar
½ tsp salt, ¼ tsp pepper, 1½ - 2 tbsp cornflour

1. Mix all the other ingredients of the balls. Add enough milk so that the mixture binds together. (Add 1 bread slice first and another one may be added if the balls fall apart on frying).
2. Make oval balls. Flatten each ball.
3. Deep fry 2-3 pieces at a time on moderately high flame. Reduce flame when the balls turn light brown. Fry on low flame till they get cooked and turn brown. Keep the balls aside.
4. To prepare Manchurian sauce, heat 2 tbsp oil. Add ginger and garlic. Fry on low flame till they start to change colour.
5. Add green chillies and onions. Cook for one minute.
6. Reduce heat and add soya sauce, tomato ketchup, vinegar, salt and pepper. Cook for 2-3 minutes.
7. Add 1½ cups of water. Boil. Keep on low flame for 2 minutes. Strain. Discard the food in the strainer. Keep the liquid aside.
8. Dissolve cornflour in ½ cup water. Keep aside.
9. Boil the strained liquid. Add cornflour stirring continuously. Cook till slightly thick. Keep the sauce aside.
10. To serve, boil the sauce. Add the balls to the Manchurian sauce and keep on low heat for one minute. Serve hot garnished with chopped spring onion greens.

Braised Mixed Vegetables

Serves 4

½ cup vegetable stock (page 31)
1 tsp finely chopped ginger
½ tsp chopped garlic
½ tsp sugar
100 gms broccoli florets
1 large onion - cut into eight pieces
100 gms green beans - cut into 1" lengths
200 gms button mushrooms
1 tbsp soya sauce
1 tbsp dry sherry
2 tsp cornflour

1. Boil stock in a pan.
2. Add ginger, garlic, sugar, broccoli, onion, beans and mushrooms. Cover, and cook on high heat for 3-4 minutes.
3. Blend soya sauce and sherry with cornflour.
4. Stir the cornflour paste into the vegetable mixture to thicken slightly. Serve at once.

Cottage Cheese (Paneer) in Garlic Sauce

Serves 3-4 *Picture on page 11*

150 gm cottage cheese *(paneer)*
2 tbsp cornflour
2 tbsp plain flour *(maida)*
¼ tsp each of pepper & salt
¼ tsp ajinomoto (optional)
4 tbsp water

GARLIC SAUCE
15 flakes garlic or 2 tsp garlic paste
1 tbsp oil
2 tbsp tomato ketchup
1 tsp soya sauce
½ tsp white pepper, ½ tsp salt
a pinch of sugar, ¼ tsp ajinomoto (optional)
3/4 cup water
1 tbsp cornflour mixed with ¼ cup water
a few spring onion greens - finely chopped for garnishing

1. To prepare the sauce, peel and grind the garlic to a smooth paste.
2. Heat oil and fry the garlic on low heat till it starts to change it's colour.
3. Add tomato ketchup, pepper, salt and soya sauce. Cook for 1 minute. Add sugar and ajinomoto.
4. Add water. Bring to a boil and simmer for 2 minutes.
5. Add cornflour paste, stirring all the time, until the sauce thickens. Remove from heat. Keep sauce aside.
6. Cut cottage cheese in big rectangular cubes.
7. Make a thick batter by mixing cornflour, plain flour, salt, pepper and ajinomoto with water.
8. Dip paneer pieces & deep fry to a golden colour.
9. At the time of serving, heat sauce. Put the cheese pieces & boil for 1-2 minutes till cheese turn soft. Transfer to a serving dish.
10. Garnish with spring onion greens and serve with fried rice.

Eggplant in Szechwan Ginger Sauce

Serves 4

GINGER SAUCE
2 tbsp oil
1 tbsp chopped ginger
1 tsp garlic
2 - 3 dry, red chillies
½ cup tomato juice
1 tsp chilli sauce
½ cup tomato ketchup
1/3 cup water
2 tsp soya sauce
¼ tsp each of sugar
¼ tsp ajinomoto (optional)
3 tsp cornflour
½ tsp salt

FRIED EGGPLANT
1 eggplant - cut into ½" thick slices lengthwise & then into fingers
3/4 cup plain flour *(maida)*
½ tsp salt, 1 tbsp oil
¼ tsp baking powder
oil for deep frying

1. Rub salt an eggplant fingers & keep aside for 20-30 minutes. Rinse with cold water & dry them well with kitchen napkin.
2. Mix plain flour, salt and baking powder. Add 3/4-1 cup water to get a batter of a thick coating consistency. Add oil & blend well.
3. Dip eggplant slices in batter and deep fry to a golden colour. Keep fried brinjals aside.
4. In a frying pan heat oil. Reduce heat and add broken dried chillies.
5. Add garlic. Fry for 1 minute.
6. Mix in ginger. Further fry for 1 minute.
7. Reduce heat and add soya sauce and chilli sauce. Mix for a few seconds.
8. Add tomato juice, tomato ketchup and water. Stirring it, bring to a boil and cook for 2 - 3 minutes.
9. Add salt, sugar and ajinomoto.
10. Mix cornflour dissolved in ¼ cup water. Cook till thick. Remove from fire. Keep sauce aside.
11. At the time of serving, heat the sauce and add the fried brinjals.

Vegetable with Almonds

Serves 4

2 spring onions
¼ of a cucumber
1 capsicum
1 parboiled carrot - cut into flowers
4-5 medium florets of cauliflower - parboiled
¼ cup boiled shelled peas
5 tbsp oil
½ tsp ajinomoto (optional)
½ tsp white pepper
salt to taste
3/4 cup water
1 tsp sugar
10-15 almonds
2 tbsp cornflour mixed with ½ cup water
1 tsp chilli sauce

1. Cut all vegetables into big pieces.
2. Boil, blanch (remove skin) and split almonds.
3. Heat oil and fry almonds to a golden colour. Keep aside.
4. Add vegetables and stir fry with salt, pepper and ajinomoto.
5. Add chilli sauce, water and sugar. Boil.
6. Add cornflour paste and cook for one minute.
7. Put some almonds and mix, keeping aside a few for garnishing.
8. Put few almonds on top at the time of serving.

Vegetable HongKong with Fried Noodles

Picture on facing page *Serves 4*

VEGETABLE HONGKONG
3-4 medium florets of cauliflower - parboiled
1 carrot - cut into leaves - parboiled
5-6 french beans - parboiled
2-3 leaves of cabbage - torn into big pieces
1 capsicum - cut into big pieces
1 spring onion - quartered
1 tsp finely chopped garlic or ginger
2-3 dry red chillies - broken into pieces
¼ pinches ajinomoto (optional), ½ tsp sugar, salt and pepper to taste
2 tbsp soya sauce, 2 tsp vinegar, 2 tsp chilli sauce
1½ tbsp cornflour dissolved in 1 cup water
3 tbsp oil
2-3 tbsp walnuts or cashewnuts

FRIED NOODLES
2 cups boiled noodles
2 tbsp oil
½ tsp salt
¼ tsp ajinomoto (optional)
¼ tsp red chilli powder
1 tbsp soya sauce

1. Heat 3 tbsp oil in a wok or a frying pan. Reduce heat. Add nuts. Fry to a golden colour on low flame. Remove from pan.
2. Add ginger or garlic to the oil. Cook for ½ minute.
3. Add red chillies, vegetables & ajinomoto. Stir fry over a high flame for 2 minutes.
4. Add the soya sauce, vinegar, chilli sauce, salt, pepper and sugar.
5. Add cornflour paste, stirring continuously. Cook till the sauce thickens and coats the vegetables. Keep aside.
6. To prepare the fried noodles, heat 2 tbsp oil in a clean wok. Reduce heat. Add salt, ajinomoto and chilli powder. Mix. Add soya sauce and stir for a few seconds. Add boiled noodles. Fry turning occasionally, till the noodles are evenly browned.
7. Add more soya sauce if a darker colour is desired. Remove from fire.
8. To serve, place the vegetables in the centre of a plate and surround them with fried noodles. Garnish the vegetables with fried nuts.

Eggplant with Bean Curd & Basil

Serves 6

2 tbsp oil
1 tsp chopped garlic
225 gms firm bean curd (tofu), cut in 3/4" cubes
1 medium eggplant - peeled and cut into 3/4" cubes
4 ripe tomatoes - peeled and quartered
½ tsp sugar, ¼ tsp dried basil
½ tsp salt, ¼ tsp pepper
½ cup vegetable stock (page 91) or water

1. Heat oil in a wok. Lightly fry garlic and bean curd.
2. Add eggplant. Stir fry for 1 minute.
3. Add tomatoes, sugar, basil, salt, pepper and stock. Bring to a boil, then simmer gently until eggplant is tender.
4. The mixture may be thickened slightly with cornflour if preferred.

Note : Paneer may be substituted for bean curd.

Stir-Fried Bean Sprouts

Serves 4

300 gm bean sprouts
3 tbsp oil
1 thin slice fresh ginger - finely chopped
1 green pepper - sliced
1 medium onion - sliced
6-8 mushrooms - cut into thin slices
1 tsp cornflour dissolved in ¼ cup water

1. Pour boiling water over bean sprouts and let stand for 20 seconds.
2. Refresh in cold running water, drain and dry. Heat oil in a wok. Add ginger and stir-fry for 30 seconds. Add green pepper and onion. Stir-fry for 1½ minutes.
3. Add bean sprouts and mushroom slices and stir-fry for 1-2 minutes.
4. Add cornflour paste and stir fry for a few seconds. Remove from heat and serve.

Rice & Noodles

Perfect Boiled Rice

- Good quality parboiled rice (sela) should be used. Long grained rice is better.
- 1 cup uncooked rice will give about 2½ cups cooked rice.
- To boil rice, clean and wash 1½ cups rice. Soak rice for 10 minutes.
- Boil 6 cups of water with 2 tsp salt. Add rice.
- Cook, uncovered, over a medium flame, stirring occasionally, until the rice is just tender but not overcooked.
- Drain the rice and let it stand in the strainer for sometime. Fluff with a fork. Spread on a tray and cool under a fan to separate the rice grains.
- About 4 cups of cooked rice is ready. The rice should be boiled 2-3 hours before making fried rice. Hot rice when stir fried tends to get mushy.

Chinese Steamed Rice

1 cup uncooked long grained rice
2 cups water
1 tsp salt, 1 tbsp refined oil

- Clean and wash rice thoroughly.
- Heat water with salt and oil. When it boils, add the rice.
- Slow down the fire, keep a griddle (tava) under the pan of rice & cook for about 15 minutes, until soft and dry.
- Remove from fire and allow to cool. Separate the grains with a fork. Serve.

Perfect Boiled Noodles

100 gm noodles
6 cups water
1 tsp salt
2 tsp oil

- In a large pan, boil 6 cups water with 1 tsp salt and 1 tsp oil.
- Add noodles to boiling water.
- Cook uncovered, on high flame for about 2-3 minutes only.
- Remove from fire before they get overcooked. Drain.
- Wash with cold water several times.
- Strain. Leave them in the strainer for 15-20 minutes, turning them upside down, once after about 10 minutes to ensure complete drying. Apply 1 tsp oil on the noodles and keep aside till further use.

Crispy Noodles

Serves 4

100 gms noodles - boiled
1 tbsp flour
2 cups oil for frying

1. Boil noodles as given on page 102.
2. Sprinkle flour on noodles to absorb any water present.
3. Heat about 2 cups of oil. Add half of the noodles.
4. Stir, turning sides till noodles are golden in colour and form a nest like appearance. Remove from oil.
5. Drain on absorbent paper. Fry the left over noodles in the same way. Cool and store in an air tight tin.

Chicken Fried Rice

Serves 4

1 cup uncooked rice
3 tbsp oil
1 onion - finely chopped, 2 green chillies - chopped
½ tsp ajinomoto (optional)
¼ of a cabbage - thinly sliced and chopped finely
1 carrot - finely chopped
½ cup boiled, shredded chicken
½ tsp pepper powder, 2 tsp salt, ½ tsp sugar
2-3 tsp soya sauce
2 spring onions - diced

1. Wash rice. Soak in water for half an hour. Cook in chicken stock or water.
2. When the rice gets done, strain and spread on a tray. Cool under a fan. Rice should remain separate.
3. Heat oil in a wok and fry onions till very light brown. Add green chillies and ajinomoto. Add cabbage and carrot and stir fry for 1-2 minutes.
4. Add boiled shredded chicken. Saute for a minute. Add salt and sugar.
5. Add 2-3 tsp soya sauce. Mix well. Add rice. Mix well. Add pepper powder.
6. Add spring onions. Mix well, stir fry for a few seconds and remove from fire. Serve hot.

Fried Noodles with Chicken & Vegetables

Serves 4

200 gm egg noodles
oil for deep frying
1 whole chicken breast - skinned and boned
225 gm uncooked shrimp - peeled
1 clove garlic - crushed
1 piece bamboo shoot - shredded
6 Chinese mushrooms - soaked in warm water for 20 minutes and sliced
100 gm vegetables (e.g. celery, green onions, beans), cut into match sticks
½ cup chicken stock (page 01)
½ tsp cornflour
1 tbsp soya sauce
a pinch of five-spice powder (recipe given below)

5 SPICE POWDER
(Grind together to a fine powder in equal quantities, store the excess)
peppercorns
cinnamon
cloves
fennel
star anise

1. Divide noodles into four portions. Deep-fry each portion in hot oil until golden brown. Drain on paper towels.
2. Cut chicken meat into strips. Heat wok, add 1 tbsp oil and stir-fry chicken and shrimp with garlic for about 3-4 minutes, till cooked.
3. Add bamboo shoots, mushrooms and vegetable sticks. Stir fry for 2-3 minutes.
4. Pour in stock, cornflour dissolved in soya sauce and five-spice powder and simmer for 5 minutes.
4. To serve, place noodles on a plate and spoon chicken and vegetables on top.

Shrimp Egg Rice

Serves

500 gms long or medium grained rice
2 eggs
100 gms cleaned shrimps
2 spring onions
1 large onion - peeled and sliced finely
2 cloves garlic - crushed and chopped
2-3 green chillies - chopped
2 tbsp soya sauce
4 tbsp oil
1 tsp sugar
a pinch ajinomoto (optional)
¼ tsp pepper powder
juice of 1 lemon

1. Wash rice and boil.
2. Drain out water and spread the rice on a serving tray and separate the grains with a fork.
3. Squeeze lemon juice over the rice and cool under a fan.
4. Beat eggs in a bowl and season with a pinch of salt and pepper.
5. Heat the wok and add 1 tbsp oil. Add the onions and green chillies and stir fry for 2 minutes.
6. Add the beaten eggs. Allow to set slightly and then stir the mixture until it scrambles. Remove on to a plate.
7. Heat wok and add 1 tbsp oil. Fry the garlic for 1 minute. Then add shrimps and cook for 2 minutes. Remove on to a plate.
8. Heat wok and add the remaining oil, a little salt, pepper and cooked rice. Stir fry to heat.
9. Stir in soya sauce, shrimp, egg mixture and sugar.
10. Add spring onions, stirring the mixture to blend. Serve hot.

Haka Noodles with Vegetables

Serves 4

FRIED NOODLES

100 gm noodles - boiled (page 102)
2 tbsp oil
3 dry whole red chillies - broken into bits
½ tsp chilli powder, 2 tsp soya sauce
½ tsp salt

VEGETABLES

1 capsicum - shredded
1 carrot - shredded
½ cup shredded cabbage - soaked in warm water for 20 minutes
3-4 flakes garlic - crushed and chopped (optional)
2-3 spring onions or 1 ordinary onion
2 tbsp shredded bamboo shoots (optional)
3-4 tbsp bean sprouts (optional)
1-2 tbsp dried mushrooms
½ tsp each of salt and pepper
½ tsp sugar, ½ tsp ajinomoto (optional)
1 tbsp soya sauce, 2 tsp vinegar
1 cup water, 1½ tbsp cornflour dissolved in ½ cup water

1. In a pan, heat 2 tbsp oil. Remove from fire, add broken red chillies and chilli powder.
2. Return to fire and mix in the boiled noodles, salt and soya sauce. Fry for 1 minute, till evenly brown in colour.
3. Keep the fried noodles aside.
4. To prepare the vegetables, shred all vegetables.
5. Heat 3 tbsp oil. Reduce heat & add garlic.
6. Add vegetables in sequence of their tenderness - onions, sprouts, bamboo shoots, mushrooms, capsicum, carrot and cabbage.
7. Add ajinomoto, salt and pepper. Add soya sauce and vinegar. Cook for ½ minute.
8. Add water. Boil.
9. Add cornflour mixture, stirring continuously. Cook for 1 minute till thick. Remove from fire.
10. To serve, spread the fried noodles on a platter.
11. Pour the prepared hot vegetables over the noodles. Serve.

Chicken Haka Noodles

Serves 4

3 tbsp oil
1 tsp chilli powder
4-5 flakes garlic - crushed
200 gms shredded chicken
2-3 spring onions - shredded diagonally
3-4 tbsp bean sprouts
2 tbsp shredded bamboo
1 tbsp shredded mushrooms
1 capsicum - shredded
1 medium sized carrot - shredded
50 gms cabbage - shredded
2 tbsp soya sauce
2 tsp vinegar
1 cup chicken stock
½ tsp each of salt, sugar & pepper
½ tsp ajinomoto (optional)
1-2 tbsp cornflour dissolved in ½ cup water

NOODLES
100 gms noodles
½ tsp chilli powder, ½ tsp salt
2 dried red chillies, 2 tsp soya sauce
3-4 tbsp oil

1. Shred the vegetables. In a frying pan, heat 3 tbsp oil, reduce heat and add chilli powder. Add garlic. Add the chicken pieces. Fry to a pale colour.
2. Stir fry in sequence - onion, bean sprouts, bamboo shoots, mushrooms, capsicum, carrot and cabbage. Reduce heat and add the stock and all the other ingredients, except cornflour paste.
3. Give one boil and add cornflour paste. Cook till the sauce turns thick. Remove from fire and keep aside.
4. To boil the noodles, boil 5-6 cups water with 1 tsp salt. Boil the noodles in salted water for 3-4 minutes. Drain the water. Put the noodles under running water. Rub a little oil over the noodles.
5. In a frying pan heat oil, reduce heat, add broken chillies & then chilli powder. Mix in the boiled noodles. Add salt & soya sauce. Stir fry for 2 minutes.
6. To serve, put noodles on a platter. Pour warm vegetables over it.

American Chopsuey with Vegetables

Picture on facing page **Serves 4**

100 gm crispy noodles (recipe on page 103)
1 carrot - parboiled
8 french beans - parboiled
1 green chilli - shredded
1 capsicum - shredded
1 onion - shredded
3/4 cup cabbage - shredded
½ cup bean sprouts
2 cups water
5 tbsp oil
¼ tsp ajinomoto (optional)
½ tsp white pepper
4 tbsp tomato ketchup
salt to taste
1 tsp vinegar
1 tsp soya sauce
3 tbsp cornflour dissolved in ½ cup water

1. Prepare crispy noodles as given on page 103.
2. Scrape carrot, string french beans.
3. Parboil them by dropping the whole carrot and french beans in 2 cups of boiling water with ½ tsp salt. Strain after half a minute. Cool.
4. Shred all vegetables - capsicum, onion, cabbage, carrot and french beans.
5. Heat 5 tbsp of oil. Add sprouts and ajinomoto. Stir fry for 1 minute.
6. Add the remaining vegetables, pepper and salt. Stir fry for 2 minutes.
7. Add soya sauce, vinegar and tomato ketchup. Cook for ½ minute.
8. Add water. Bring to a boil.
9. Add cornflour paste, stirring continuously. Cook for about 2 minutes, till thick. Keep aside.
10. To serve, spread crispy noodles on a serving platter, keeping aside a few for the top.
11. Top with the prepared vegetables.
12. Sprinkle some left over crispy noodles on it.
13. Serve hot.

Fried Rice with Mushrooms & Bamboo Shoots

Serves 4

1½ cups uncooked rice
6 cups water
½ cup sliced mushrooms
½ cup sliced bamboo shoots
4 spring onions
1 cup finely chopped spring onion tops
3 tbsp oil
¼ tsp ajinomoto (optional)
2-3 tbsp soya sauce
salt to taste

1. Boil and drain the rice as explained on page 102.
2. Peel the onions and cut into thin rings.
3. Heat oil. Stir fry the onions, mushrooms, bamboo shoots, ajinomoto and salt over high flame for 3 minutes.
4. Add the rice, soya sauce and spring onion tops.
5. Stir fry over a high flame for 2 to 3 minutes.
6. Serve hot.

American Chopsuey with Chicken

Serves 4

2 tbsp oil
2 flakes of garlic - crushed
2-3 spring onions - chopped
2-3 mushrooms - shredded
3 tbsp bean sprouts
1 medium sized carrot - shredded
6-7 tbsp shredded cabbage
50 gms each of shredded chicken, prawns and ham (increase quantity of the other two if omitting any one)
¼ tsp each of salt and ajinomoto (optional), ½ tsp sugar
2 tbsp soya sauce, 4 tbsp tomato ketchup
1 tsp sherry/gin, 1 cup chicken stock
3 tsp cornflour

TOPPING
1 egg - fried

CRISPY NOODLES (PAGE 103)
100 gms chow noodles
oil for deep frying

1. Deep fry the noodles in two batches, in hot smoking oil until crisp & golden brown as given on page 103. Keep aside.
2. In a wok, heat oil, saute garlic. Add chicken, ham and prawns.
3. Fry to a pale colour. Stir fry in sequence - spring onions, bean sprouts, bamboo shoots, carrot, cabbage.
4. Reduce heat and add chicken stock, sauces and seasonings. Cook for 2 minutes.
5. Mix cornflour with water and add to make a thick sauce. Further cook for 2-3 minutes till thick.
6. In a serving dish, put the crispy noodles (noodles fried in oil). Pour the meat & vegetables on the crispy noodles. Place a fried egg on top.
7. Serve hot garnished with chopped spring onions.

Chinese Chicken Chopsuey

Remove tomato ketchup from the vegetables and do not place a fried egg on the top.

Chinese Vegetable Chop Suey

(without tomato ketchup)

Serves 4

100 gm crispy noodles (page 103)
1 carrot - parboiled
8 french beans - parboiled
3/4 cup shredded cabbage
1 capsicum - shredded
½ cup small florets of cauliflower
2 spring onions - quartered
½ cup bean sprouts
5 tbsp oil
¼ tsp ajinomoto (optional)
1 tsp white pepper
1 tsp sugar
2 cups water
1½ tbsp soya sauce
salt to taste
2½ tbsp cornflour mixed with 1/3 cup water

1. Prepare crispy noodles as given on page 103.
1. Scrape the carrot, string the french beans, remove the seeds from the capsicum and peel the onions.
2. Drop the whole carrot and french beans into 2 cups of boiling water to which ½ tsp salt has been added.
3. Boil for ½ minute, drain and cool. Shred beans diagonally and carrots into match sticks.
4. Shred capsicum and quarter the onions.
5. Heat 5 tbsp oil in an iron pan and stir fry the cauliflower, spring onions, bean sprouts and ajinomoto over a high flame for 2 minutes.
6. Add the remaining vegetables, pepper, sugar and salt.
7. Stir fry over a high flame for 2 minutes.
8. Add soya sauce. Cook for ½ minute. Add water.
9. Bring to a boil and add cornflour mixed with 1/3 cup water, stirring all the time, until thickened. Remove from fire.
10. To serve, put the crispy noodles at the bottom of a serving bowl and top with the vegetable mixture.
11. Alternatively, serve the crispy noodles and vegetables mixture side by side in a dish.

Fried Noodles with Mushrooms & Bean Sprouts

Serves 4

100 gm boiled noodles - page 102
3 tbsp oil
2 spring onions - chopped finely
½ cup bean sprouts
2 capsicums - sliced finely
1 cup small white fresh mushrooms
2 tbsp soya sauce
1 tbsp vinegar
a pinch of each - salt, pepper and ajinomoto (optional)

1. Heat 1 tbsp oil. Add the noodles and fry for 1 minute till golden. Remove and keep aside.
2. Heat the remaining oil. Add the spring onions and stir fry.
3. Add the mushrooms.
4. Stir fry for 5-7 minutes till they get cooked. Add bean sprouts & capsicum. Stir fry for 1 minute.
5. Slide in the noodles and sprinkle with soya sauce, vinegar, salt, pepper and ajinomoto.
6. Toss well with a fork so that all the ingredients are mixed well.
7. Transfer onto a serving dish and serve hot.

Fried Rice with Bean Sprouts & Nuts

Serves 4

1½ cups uncooked rice
6 cups water
2½ cups bean sprouts
4 spring onions
1 cup finely chopped spring onion tops
¼ cup raw skinless peanuts
¼ cup shelled walnuts
6 tbsp oil
¼ tsp ajinomoto (optional)
2-3 tbsp soya sauce
salt to taste

1. Boil and drain rice as explained on page 102.
2. Peel and chop the onions very finely.
3. Heat oil. Fry the walnuts and peanuts until golden brown. Drain and set aside.
4. Sprinkle a pinch of salt on the nuts if desired.
5. Heat the remaining oil in an iron wok and stir fry the onions, bean sprouts, ajinomoto and salt over a high flame for 3 to 4 minutes.
6. Add the rice, soya sauce and spring onion tops.
7. Stir fry over a high flame for 3 to 4 minutes.
8. Garnish the rice with the fried nuts and serve.

Vegetable Party Fried Rice

Serves 4

1½ cups uncooked long grain rice
6 cups water
4 tbsp oil
1 tomato - chopped
¼ cup sliced mushrooms
¼ cup carrot - diced
¼ cup parboiled french beans - diced
¼ cup diced capsicum
¼ cup shelled green peas - boiled
1 cup finely chopped spring onion tops
2 tbsp soya sauce
1 tbsp fried almonds
1 tbsp fried walnuts
2 tbsp pineapple cubes (tinned pineapple)
¼ tsp ajinomoto (optional)
salt to taste

1. Wash rice. Boil water with 1 tsp salt. Add rice. Cook, uncovered, over a medium flame, stirring occasionally, until the rice is just tender, but not overcooked. Strain. Cool the rice for 2 hours.
2. Peel and chop onions finely.
3. Heat oil and add 1 chopped tomato, mince fry.
4. Stir fry the mushrooms, over a high flame for 2 minutes.
5. Add all the vegetables, except onion tops and peas. Add ajinomoto and salt.
6. Add the rice, soya sauce, spring onion tops and green peas.
7. Stir fry over a high flame for 3 to 5 minutes.
8. Garnish rice with pineapple cubes, fried almonds, and walnuts.

Vegetable Chow Mein

Serves 4

100 gm noodles
2-3 flakes garlic - crushed (optional)
1 onion - shredded
1 capsicum - shredded
1 cup shredded cabbage
1 carrot - shredded
¼ tsp ajinomoto (optional)
1 tsp white pepper
a pinch sugar
2 tsp soya sauce
1 tbsp vinegar
1½ tsp chilli sauce
2 tbsp oil
3/4 tsp salt

1. Boil noodles and dry them as given on page 102.
2. Shred all vegetables into thin long strips. To shred onions, peel and cut into half. Cut each half into thin semi circles to get thin long strips of onion.
3. Heat oil. Add garlic. Add onions. Stir fry for ½ minute.
4. Stir fry carrots and capsicum for ½ minute. Add cabbage.
5. Add salt, pepper, sugar & ajinomoto.
6. Add boiled noodles. Add soya sauce and mix well.
7. Add vinegar & chilli sauce. Stir fry for 1 minute. Add more soya sauce for a darker colour. Serve.

Vegetable Fried Rice

Serves 4 *Picture on page 11*

1½ cups uncooked rice
2 tbsp oil
2 green chillies - chopped finely
2 green onions - chopped
2 flakes garlic - crushed & chopped (optional)
¼ cup very finely sliced french beans
1 carrot - finely diced
½ big capsicum - diced
salt, pepper, ajinomoto (optional) - ½ tsp of each
1-2 tsp soya sauce (according to the colour desired)
1 tsp vinegar (optional)

1. Boil rice as given on page 102. Strain and spread out on a tray and keep under the fan for the rice to dry out.
1. Chop green onions, keeping the chopped green part separate.
2. Heat oil. Splutter green chillies.
3. Stir fry garlic and onions, leaving the green part.
4. Add beans, then carrots. Stir fry for 1 minute. Add capsicum.
5. Add salt, pepper & ajinomoto.
6. Add rice. Add soya sauce, vinegar & chilli sauce.
7. Add the green onions and salt to taste. Stir fry the rice for 2 minutes.
8. Serve hot.

Pork Fried Rice with Almonds

Serves 6

250 gms lean pork - thinly sliced
1 tbsp soya sauce
1 tbsp cornflour
4 tbsp oil
4 spring onions - cut in ½ inch pieces
1 medium size capsicum - cut in fine shreds
2 cups cooked boiled rice
100 gms almonds - toasted
2 eggs - lightly beaten

1. Combine pork, soya sauce and cornflour.
2. Heat 3 tbsp oil in a wok. Add pork mixture and stir fry for 2 minutes.
3. Add half of the spring onions, capsicum and salt. Stir fry for 1 minute.
4. Add rice, almonds, stir frying to blend ingredients. Remove from heat.
5. Heat 1 tbsp oil in a wok. Pour in beaten eggs to form a flat omelette. Cook for 1 minute. Flip over and cook for further 1 minute. Remove from heat and cut into thin strips.
6. Spoon rice on to a serving dish and garnish with egg strips and remaining spring onions.

Rice Noodles Singapore Style

Serves 4

250 gm rice noodles
2 tbsp oil
2 eggs - beaten
100 gms bean sprouts
½" piece fresh ginger - shredded
100 gms cooked ham (optional)
100 gms chicken - shredded
2 flakes garlic - finely chopped
1 tbsp chicken stock (page 31)
2 tbsp soya sauce
50 gm fresh green onions - finely chopped

1. Soak the rice noodles in warm water for 10 minutes and then drain well.
2. Heat 1 tbsp oil in a frying pan or wok and make a thin pancake with the beaten eggs. Remove from pan & cut into thin strips.
3. Heat wok and add 1 tbsp oil. Fry ginger and bean sprouts for 2 minutes.
4. Add garlic, cooked ham and chicken and fry for 2 minutes.
5. Add rice noodles and stir fry for 2-3 minutes.
6. Add salt and chicken stock. Mix well.
7. Add soya sauce and stir over heat for 1 minute.
8. Top with spring onions and egg strips.

7 Jewel Rice

Serves 6

4 tbsp oil
3 cups boiled rice
1 tbsp soya sauce
salt to taste
1 egg - beaten
¼ tsp pepper powder

SEVEN JEWELS
1 small cabbage
2 carrots - peeled, cut into 1" pieces and boiled
1 capsicum
3-4 mushrooms - halved
1 cup boneless chicken cubes - boiled
100 gms bean sprouts
10 spinach leaves or 1 firm head lettuce

DRESSING
3-4 flakes garlic - crushed
2 slices fresh ginger - grated
1 tsp sugar
1 tsp ajinomoto (optional)
1¼ tsp pepper, 1¼ tsp salt
1 cup stock
1 tbsp sherry
1 tsp soya sauce
3 tbsp cornflour - dissolved in ½ cup water

1. Heat oil in a wok over moderate heat.
2. Pour the beaten egg. Stir and add cooked rice. Sprinkle soya sauce and salt. Keep hot.
3. Cut the vegetables into 1" even sized pieces.
4. Heat oil. Add garlic and ginger. Fry for a minute.
5. Add carrots, sprouts, capsicum, cabbage, mushrooms, lettuce and chicken. Stir fry for 2-3 minutes.
6. Add sugar, ajinomoto, pepper, salt and stock. Add soya sauce & sherry. Boil for 1-2 minutes.
7. Add cornflour paste. Stir well till it thickens. Remove dressing from fire.
8. Arrange the hot rice on a serving plate and spoon the dressing on top.

Note : For a vegetarian version, use paneer cubes instead of chicken.

Desserts

Toffee Apples

Picture on facing page

Serves 6

3 delicious golden or red apples
½ cup plain flour *(maida)*
2 tbsp cornflour
½ tsp baking powder

CARAMEL COATING
1 cup sugar
2 tbsp oil
½ cup water
2 tsp sesame (*til*) seeds
oil for deep frying

1. Put the sugar, 2 tbsp oil and ½ cup of water in a pan or a kadhai and cook on a high flame.
2. When the mixture begins to boil, reduce heat and stir continuously to melt the sugar.
3. Continue stirring the syrup for about 5 minutes after the first boil or until it is light golden in colour and feels sticky when felt between the thumb and the fore finger. It forms a thread when the finger is pulled apart.
4. Remove from the heat, add the sesame seeds and mix well. Keep the caramel syrup aside.
5. Mix the plain flour, cornflour and baking powder in a bowl. Add enough water, about ½ cup to get a smooth, thick batter of a coating consistency.
6. Peel and cut the apples into four pieces. If the apples are big you can cut them into 8 pieces. Remove the seeds.
7. Heat oil for frying. Coat the apple pieces evenly with the batter and deep fry 5-6 pieces together at one time, in hot oil until golden.
8. Keep a serving bowl filled with ice-cubes ready and cover with water.
9. Put the fried apples in the caramel syrup and coat evenly. Drain well and dip immediately into the ice-cubes bowl. Keep for a few minutes till the caramel coating hardens.
10. Drain thoroughly. Keep aside till serving time.
11. Serve plain or with ice cream, sprinkled with some more seasame seeds

Note: You may use pears or bagugoshas too.

Assorted Fruit Fritters

Serves 8-10

1 large, firm mango - peeled
4 firm bananas - peeled
2 apples - peeled
4 slices pineapple
4-6 tbsp flour for dusting
¼ tsp cinnamon powder

BATTER
2 cups plain flour *(maida)*
1 tsp baking powder
¼ tsp salt
2/3 cup milk
2/3 cup cold water
oil for deep frying
icing sugar

1. Cut fruit into serving pieces.
2. Combine flour and cinnamon and lightly dust fruits.
3. To make the batter, sift plain flour. Add flour, baking powder and salt into a bowl.
4. Combine milk and water and beat into flour to form a smooth batter. Stir well before using.
5. Dip fruit into batter and fry in hot oil to cover until golden. Drain well.
6. Arrange on a serving platter. Sprinkle with icing sugar.

Almond and Cashew Nut Cookies

Makes About 24

1 cup shortening (*dalda ghee*)
1 cup white sugar
1 egg - beaten
3 tbsp ground almonds
3 tbsp ground cashew nuts
½ tsp vanilla extract
½ tsp almond extract
2½ cups all-purpose flour
1½ level tsp baking powder
a pinch of salt

1. Cream shortening and sugar together in a bowl. Add egg, almonds, cashews, vanilla and almond extract.
2. Sift flour, baking powder and salt together. Fold into creamed mixture and knead lightly. Shape dough into walnut sized balls. Arrange on lightly greased baking sheets. Press each ball with a fork to flatten slightly.
3. Bake at 400°F (200°C) until pale golden, 15-20 minutes.

Almond Float

Serves 4

2½ cups milk
¼ cup sugar
a few drops almond essence
2 tbsp gelatine
½ cup water
some fresh fruits and canned lychees

1. Boil milk, remove from heat and add sugar. Cool slightly then add almond essence. Sprinkle gelatine over water and leave until water is absorbed. Dissolve gelatine on low heat. Stir into milk mixture. Transfer to a rectangular dish and chill till well set.
2. When ready to serve, cut almond gelatine into diamond shapes. Place fruit in a serving bowl and arrange diamond shapes on top.

Date & Sesame Wontons

Serves 4

½ cup milk
2 tbsp powdered sugar
oil for deep frying
¼ teacup sesame seeds *(til)*
½ teacup brown sugar
½ teacup chopped dated
1 tbsp soft butter

WONTONS WRAPPERS
2 cups plain flour *(maida)*
½ tsp salt
oil for deep frying

1. To prepare the wonton wrappers, sieve the flour and salt together.
2. Add hot water gradually and make a soft dough. Knead well till smooth and keep aside for 30 minutes.
3. Knead the dough with oiled hands until it becomes smooth and elastic. Keep dough aside.
4. Toast the sesame seeds in a heavy bottomed kadhai on a medium flame until they are golden. Cool. Crush them coarsely.
5. For the stuffing, mix toasted sesame seeds with brown sugar, dates and butter.
6. Roll out wonton dough into small thin circles of 2½" diameter.
7. Place about 1 tsp of the stuffing in the centre of each wonton wrapper.
8. Pull the edges of the dough around the filling and with the help of a little milk, twist to seal like a money bag.
9. Deep fry in oil until golden. Cool.
10. Sprinkle the powdered sugar on top.
11. Serve hot with vanilla ice-cream.

Note : You can also top the wontons with warm honey and serve hot.

Date & Coconut Pancakes

Serves 4

½ cup cornflour
½ cup plain flour (*maida*)
½ cup milk
½ cup water
1 tbsp sesame seeds (*til*)
2 tsp melted butter or oil
a pinch salt
oil for frying

FILLING
½ cup grated fresh coconut
½ cup dates - deseeded and finely chopped
¼ cup powdered sugar

TO SERVE
vanilla ice-cream

1. Mix all ingredients of the filling together and keep aside.
2. Mix the cornflour, plain flour, milk, water, butter and salt into a thin pouring batter of a smooth consistency. Add sesame seeds and mix well.
3. Put 1 tsp oil onto a nonstick frying pan of about 7" diameter and keep on fire.
4. Do not make the pan too hot. Pour 1 small *karchhi*, (about 2 tbsp) of the batter in the pan and shake the pan in a circular motion so as to spread the batter evenly.
5. Cook firstly on one side until done and then on the other side.
6. Repeat with the remaining batter.
7. To serve, spread 1 tbsp of the filling on each pancake and fold. If desired, seal the edges by applying a little of the pancake mixture.
8. Fry until crisp. Cut into pieces and serve with vanilla ice cream.

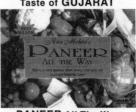